Developing Mediumship

Developing Mediumship

GORDON SMITH

HAY HOUSE

Australia • Canada • Hong Kong • India
South Africa • United Kingdom • United States

First published and distributed in the United Kingdom by:
Hay House UK Ltd, 292B Kensal Rd, London W10 5BE. Tel.: (44) 20 8962 1230;
Fax: (44) 20 8962 1239. www.hayhouse.co.uk

Published and distributed in the United States of America by:
Hay House, Inc., PO Box 5100, Carlsbad, CA 92018-5100. Tel.: (1) 760 431 7695 or
(800) 654 5126; Fax: (1) 760 431 6948 or (800) 650 5115. www.hayhouse.com

Published and distributed in Australia by:
Hay House Australia Ltd, 18/36 Ralph St, Alexandria NSW 2015. Tel.: (61) 2 9669 4299;
Fax: (61) 2 9669 4144. www.hayhouse.com.au

Published and distributed in the Republic of South Africa by:
Hay House SA (Pty), Ltd, PO Box 990, Witkoppen 2068. Tel./Fax: (27) 11 467 8904.
www.hayhouse.co.za

Published and distributed in India by:
Hay House Publishers India, Muskaan Complex, Plot No.3, B-2, Vasant Kunj,
New Delhi – 110 070. Tel.: (91) 11 4176 1620; Fax: (91) 11 4176 1630.
www.hayhouse.co.in

Distributed in Canada by:
Raincoast, 9050 Shaughnessy St, Vancouver, BC V6P 6E5. Tel.: (1) 604 323 7100;
Fax: (1) 604 323 2600

© Gordon Smith, 2009

The moral rights of the author have been asserted.

The author of this book does not dispense medical advice or prescribe the use of any
technique as a form of treatment for physical or medical problems without the advice of a
physician, either directly or indirectly. The intent of the author is only to offer information
of a general nature to help you in your quest for emotional and spiritual wellbeing. In the
event you use any of the information in this book for yourself, which is your constitutional
right, the author and the publisher assume no responsibility for your actions.

A catalogue record for this book is available from the British Library.

ISBN 978-1-84850-069-3

Printed in the UK by CPI William Clowes Ltd, Beccles, NR34 7TL.

This book is dedicated to all those who are curious about learning how to open up their spiritual awareness of themselves and of life itself.

I would like to thank Kathy Sorley for her work on the original edition of this book, as well as Paul Smith and Stella Blair for giving me the inspiration to write it.

Contents

Contents

Introduction

'Whatever you do or dream you can, begin it.
Boldness has power, genius and magic in it.'
GOETHE

Have you ever thought, 'There's got to be more to life than this?' I think most people at some stage or other in their lives do so, and usually go on to more probing musings like, 'Why am I here?' or 'What is the purpose of my life?' and 'Is there life after death?' This is particularly true for those who feel they possess psychic or mediumistic ability.

Throughout history there have always been people who have shown unique gifts and special abilities for seership, healing, telepathy and even communicating with the so-called 'dead'. You may ask, 'Is all of this just pure coincidence?' Some people would dismiss it as such, but the succession of psychically gifted people recorded throughout time seems to suggest that there are abilities that cannot yet be fully explained, and moreover that there are people who possess these abilities.

I should say up front that I am not a person who believes in coincidence. And ever since I can remember, I have been aware of a sense of something strange happening around me – a feeling, if you like, of being different, a bit unusual, aware of energies that others didn't seem to see or feel. Many psychic and telepathic experiences occurred during my early life that no one close to me seemed able to explain.

When I was a young child, these happenings frightened my mother, causing her great alarm. I was distressed to be the cause of her upset, so I learned very quickly to keep them to myself. Then, in my early twenties, after the sudden death of a close friend's brother in a house fire and his early morning visitation to me to say goodbye as he passed over into spirit, I could no longer ignore the truth of what I could see, hear and feel. Spirit was asking me to wake up.

So I took it upon myself to investigate these mystical happenings. I felt compelled to learn more. It was something I felt I just *had* to do. It was as if a voice inside me kept calling and calling until I finally answered.

Soon after committing to exploring my abilities, I set out to join a Spiritualist development circle. I literally walked the length of West Prince's Street in Glasgow three times one Thursday night, trying to find my new spiritual classroom. On the third pass by, I decided to give up if I had no success in finding the right place.

Fortunately for me, Mrs Primrose, my new spiritual teacher-to-be, was somehow moved to look outside the door one more time before starting her circle. As circumstance would have it, I was passing that door for the third and final time at that very moment. She spotted me and looked searchingly into my eyes, right through to my soul. It was then that she invited me inside. And so it was that I began my true spiritual journey.

It is my firm belief that she was *meant* to look out at that moment and I was *meant* to be there that night. I don't believe that people who are meant to work for the spirit world can ever be in the wrong place at the wrong time. Spirit ensures that this simply does not happen. Remembering how close I was to going straight home that night, and in all probability never going back, I realize that spirit made sure I was not allowed to slip by.

Despite having experienced many psychic happenings during the course of my early life, joining this circle was to be just the beginning of my real training. Those early life events turned out to be no more than mere glimpses of what I could achieve as a medium if my abilities were properly developed.

A quick word of definition here: there is a very large difference between being psychic and being mediumistic. To be psychic and to have psychic ability is to tune into an object or person here on the earth plane and see their life. To be a medium, however, is to provide a bridge for those who have crossed. For an example, if a person saw the future and it happened, that would be a psychic event, but to bring a message through from a person in the spirit world to one still living here would be the work of a medium. All mediums are psychic, but not all psychics are mediums. That's because all mediums pick up information psychically from people as well as through the spirit world.

There are actually many thousands of people all around the world who have both psychic and mediumistic gifts. However, for whatever reason, only a few make concerted and committed attempts to develop them further. If you are one of those people who is aware they might have a gift and at the very least a desire to help others with the aid of spirit, then I am writing this book especially for you.

So how do you know that you really want to be a medium? Most eventual mediums have experienced paranormal episodes throughout their lives, often starting at a very young age. Some have a calling to investigate and understand their gifts, while others wish to help others and feel this is the right way for them. Others are not sure what lies ahead for them, but would like to gain greater awareness of themselves, spirit and others and see where the journey takes them.

If you would like to explore further, then this book contains a course of possible development I have charted for you, as well as explanations of the different types of spiritual ability and what you may encounter during your development. The episodes and experiences that I went through were personal to me – you will encounter your own during your journey – but I hope they will give you an idea of what you might expect. Many of the working mediums I know and have spoken to have been on very similar journeys. If you feel called to this path and to working with spirit, in whatever capacity, I welcome you to walk it with me and invite you to take it as far as you feel spirit wants to travel with you.

The journey to realize your particular abilities and develop them to their fullest can and probably will take many years – though that time will seem to pass very quickly! Be brave enough to step onto the path and trust where that will take you. Spirit has touched you for a reason and will honour your courage to proceed. I would advise anyone who is seriously seeking to take this path to take heart and be as open as possible to what spirit has to reveal to them, though always with great humility, trust and love.

During my time in development there were far too many questions left unanswered, questions that left me puzzled, confused and often dispirited, and eventually led me to seek my own answers. It is only now, in the writing of this book, that I fully understand why I quested after the truth. Everything I learned was for a specific purpose – to aid others as best I could, in love and honesty, with the guidance of spirit to help and heal. I suspect that, in your own personal way, this will be your purpose too.

At this point, though, I feel I must say as clearly as I can that spiritual development is not suited to everyone. You first must be very sure that you really *want* to do this. To embark on this journey will bring about changes in your everyday life that you may or may not welcome, and you as a person will change, for to understand spirit is to understand and transform yourself.

That will of course affect every relationship you have. Some connections with friends and loved ones will benefit, growing stronger as a consequence of your development as a person and as a medium, while others may not. You may have relationships that will wither away from fear of your development. Many people around you, including close friends and family, may not understand your reasons for doing this, nor the special energy and dedication it requires. People who are sceptical or religious extremists will also doubt you, openly question you or try to thwart your work. Worse still, some will claim your actions are nonsensical or even evil. You will need to be resilient in the face of such doubts and sure that you are acting out of love.

I must also say that people of a nervous disposition or those dealing with major traumas in their lives would be better suited to joining a relaxation course or a meditation group before seeking out a development circle or embarking on any course that develops spiritual awareness. Why? For the simple reason that spiritual development takes you through an intensive examination of your mind, self and emotions before you even begin looking into the external world of spirit. It is not a quick path and the terrain can occasionally seem gruelling along the way. So, if you are already facing trauma or disruption or have fears to deal with first, now is not the time for it. Be gentle with yourself and take some time to be still. That in itself can be of great help in your life. The first part of this book will give you some ideas on how to go about this.

So, if you are aware of some of the possible obstacles and you still want to embark on the path, then please do take the next step on your journey. If inside you there is a voice, however small, calling to you, encouraging you to meet these situations and to challenge convention, then go boldly forward. If you cannot help but follow that voice, then the quest to broaden your mental horizons and develop your spiritual mediumship, not to mention discover your own true self and spiritual nature, has already begun.

STAGE ONE
BEING STILL

*'In peace there's nothing so becomes a man
As modest stillness and humility...'*
SHAKESPEARE

This very first stage on your journey is all about you. It's about finding out if this path really is for you.

It is also about learning how to be still and to relax. By learning how to be still, you will be changing – for the better. You'll be healing your mind, stripping away the layers of feeling and fear that cloud your thoughts. And once your mind is free, you can be clear about the way forward in your spiritual development. You may decide to attend a meditation circle to relax your body and mind. You may decide to develop your healing abilities. Or to develop mediumship. Wherever your journey takes you, spiritual development is all about transforming *yourself*. It can give you a bigger view of life and leave you less afraid to die, but more importantly less afraid to *live*.

1
The Beginning

'We are shaped by our thoughts; we become what we think. When the mind is pure, joy follows like a shadow that never leaves.'
THE BUDDHA

The development of spiritual awareness begins with ourselves. When we learn to love ourselves for who we are, warts and all, we develop compassion for ourselves and, naturally leading on from that, compassion for others. Developing that compassion is a wonderful thing in many ways, and one of them is that it will naturally make us more psychic. Being psychic is actually part of our nature – feeling for other people, feeling their pain, feeling their joys, being aware of what's happening in their lives. But first we have to know ourselves – to *find* ourselves, because we've so often lost ourselves along the way.

It's in finding yourself that you'll discover all your qualities – all those amazing qualities that you haven't yet tapped into. They will be there – you just don't know it yet!

And so you can learn to heal yourself. And to actually love yourself.

A very large part of developing mediumship is simply becoming aware of who you are and being able to get past that. That's because you are the instrument of this work – the means by which it passes through. Some mediums are so caught up in themselves that they give messages about their own life to other people, and very often they're actually correct, because associations from our own life can be relevant and healing for others. But there's a big difference between those messages and spirit messages. If you are clear, then you can bring spirit messages through. If you're not, you'll still in some way be focused on yourself. To be a true medium, you have to go beyond that.

But finding and accepting yourself is valuable even if you don't go on to practise mediumship. It can help you whatever you do in life. And through it you will be able to expand your consciousness and gain greater awareness of the world around you.

Using your Senses

Each of us can expand our consciousness in some way. We have five human senses and none of us really uses them to their fullest. We tend to drift through life not really being aware of who we are, where we are or what's going on around us. It's all too easy to focus on certain things, to get caught up in life's dramas, and not notice the rest. We forget to look at the beauties of the world as well as the horrors.

One of the reasons why we spend our days in this blinkered state is that we're afraid of really being engaged in life. That's what we're all frightened of when it comes down to it. Because it means taking more responsibility for ourselves and our actions. So many of us lack confidence in ourselves and believe we're not up to that, but developing our spiritual awareness will give us the strength to become more fully involved – to live our lives rather than sleepwalk through them.

Really using your five senses can be a revelation at first. Recognizing that there are other people out there who feel the same way you do at times can be very reassuring. You also begin to recognize that there's more to life than your little fishbowl – you gain a sense of being connected to something greater, something bigger, a huge flow of life that you never even knew existed.

And a great side effect of learning to recognize life in all forms is that your sense of optimism will change too – your sense of positivity. Whatever's happening to you, you'll start to live a more positive life.

It's all good, so how do you go about it? Quite simply, it's using all your senses together that develops that awareness. It's really looking at other people, really being able to tune in to them and know them. It's using more than the five physical senses of the human body – it's using a sixth sense that just 'knows'. It's listening to your inner voice.

The Inner Voice

We all have an inner voice – a voice that connects to our higher self. It's the voice we hear when we're just about to do something stupid – but we do it anyway! It's the voice that nags us to call someone because we 'just know' there's something wrong with them.

People so often hear it and ignore it, but it's the part of us that can connect to higher forces and we would do well to take notice of it. Some people put it down to spirits talking to them, but it's actually their own voice.

If we still ourselves we can learn to connect to our own voice, to connect to ourselves. A lot of people lose contact with their inner voice and look to other beings to guide them in life – whether other people or higher beings they call upon. But you have to let your inner voice guide you. It will help you through daily life, heal you and allow you to recognize your true self.

When we do that, when we recognize who we are spiritually, those on the other side can recognize us too and then we can build up links with the spirit world. But if we don't know who we are, if we're not grounded in ourselves, we won't be able to make that connection. That's another reason why the vital first step is to get to know our own selves.

A Place to Develop

When you feel ready to take this first step, the first and most important thing to consider is a place to develop. Do you need a group? Can this be practised alone?

Over my years in developing mediumship I have found that the best way is to find people who already have some experience of working spiritually. A group will provide a support network, guidance and a much wider range of experience than you would encounter alone.

Joining a group is best achieved by finding a Spiritualist church or similar organization and simply asking. If they themselves do not hold classes in development, they should be able to point you in the direction of somewhere reputable that does. As in all things that matter in life, it pays to look around and to find somewhere that feels right for you.

While it is best to approach a Spiritualist church in the United Kingdom, you may live in a country where Spiritualist churches and organizations are rare. Luckily, with the internet we now have an incredible scope of information at our fingertips and there is an appendix at the back of this book that may help you.

If you do have trouble finding a group near you, do what the first Spiritualists did: host a circle. Find some like-minded friends and start a group of your own. You can have a circle of three or more; in my first circle there were six people. As a guide, there should ideally be no more than 12 members, as more will prove difficult for one person to lead at any one time.

In any instance, it is far better to work in a group than by yourself. While you can start your development alone, you will not get far without the guidance of others with similar experience.

Development Circles

Wherever you are, there is likely to be a variety of different groups available, though collectively they are known as 'circles'.

Open and Closed Circles

There are two types of circle: 'open' and 'closed'. *Open* means a development circle where all are welcome, so from week to week different sitters can take part. A *closed* circle is much more intimate and private and usually contains members who have had some experience with spirit, attend every week and have formed a link and a bond of trust between themselves.

Normally you start off in an open circle and are then invited by the leader of the closed circle into that group. Often closed circles are held in a person's home, rather than at a church or similar Spiritualist organization. However, open circles exist all over the world and, as the name suggests, are open to all. (In the UK particularly, the Spiritualist National Union, the SNU, advertises open circles through its individual church listings. The SNU's details can be found in the appendix at the back of this book.) I initially started in an open development group that was held in a Spiritualist church.

The primary difference between circles is the number of members that can belong to a circle. While with a closed circle there can be around a dozen attending every week, in an open circle there can be as many as 50 or 60 members, each with different availability and attendance.

However, because of that level of availability – i.e. they are often unable to make a circle meeting week in, week out – numbers may vary from week to week. So there is flexibility for those wishing to develop.

Be Comfortable

The choice of circle depends very much on you. Whether you travel to a circle or attend one close to you, whether you stay in an open one or progress to a closed one, try to find one that suits your personality best.

Wherever you start out, it is important for you to know that you are developing in the safety of a properly controlled group, led by a caring and nurturing person. Make sure that you feel really comfortable with this group. Try to measure all the things going on around you with a bit of grace, and above all common sense. Development groups really do differ, and go through their own changes and growth all the time, so try to connect with one that feels good and right. Your inner feelings, your instinct, your 'gut' if you like, will tell you if you are in the right place.

If you are not happy with a circle or one becomes unsuitable for you, you are free to find another one at any time. A circle thrives on positive energy and will not function well with unhappy members.

Do not sit in a large open circle if this will make you feel uncomfortable. Private circles are more difficult to gain access to, but if you get the chance, development seems to be more accelerated in these more intimate groups, largely because of the intensity of spiritual energy and conditions that build between the sitters and the familiarity that sitters have with one another from week to week.

Remember that if you cannot find a group that feels right but you find one or more like-minded individuals, you are very welcome to start a circle of your own.

Recently, I gave a seminar in Germany to a group of people who wanted to develop mediumship. It was clear from the beginning that they had very little experience and would not benefit from teachings in mediumistic practices, so instead I worked with them on some simple practices of relaxation and meditation. I found that this was much more beneficial and the group was happy to start from the beginning and learn the basics. I then explained how they could build their own circles and by the end of the seminar they had decided to form a circle and had agreed to meet in one of their homes each week and carry on the simple practices I had taught.

While you search for a group, or search for people to start your own, you can still start your development. I have been asked how far you can progress alone, especially by those who seem unable to find a group. You *can* make a little headway, and it certainly won't hurt to try some exercises, especially those focused on relaxation and meditation, as the German group did.

Meditation

Whether or not you are sitting in a development circle, I always feel that it is good to learn to meditate. The practice of mediation is something that anyone can include in their life. It is something that can be done on your own or with others if you choose.

Meditation is simply turning your mind away from the stesses of the world and journeying within yourself. It's one of the simplest things to do – you don't have to get into strange contortions or spend three hours preparing a room or live a life of abstinence. (Unless you want to.) But you do first of all need to recognize that it's not difficult. Some people, when faced with something new, will see all the difficulties and it's too easy to think of meditation as some strange Eastern practice which involves twisting the body into all sorts of contorted states or being in the same position for hours and having to think of nothing. And how can you actually do that? Even thinking of nothing is still thinking, isn't it?

Don't worry, you don't have to tie yourself up in physical or metaphysical knots. When we meditate, we are exercising our mind, that's all.

To most people, the mind is where they think or pray in private, where they dream, imagine or worry about life. It's very seldom seen as a place to find understanding or peace, yet for spiritual seekers it is most important to become used to the inner self and learn more about it and find that peace. And we can all do it, though few people ever take time in their busy lives to try to quiet the mind or contemplate on a deeper level, or even just quietly take stock of where they are in their life at that particular moment.

Mediation also puts us in touch with the spirit within. And from there we start to expand our mind and connect to our higher consciousness. When we close our human part down and let our spiritual part come to the fore, we reconnect to the whole spiritual flow of life. We still our mind, still our body and let spirit take over. That's all there is to it.

I truly believe that it is very good for anyone who wants to embark on a spiritual journey to learn about their inner world. It really can help us to understand more about who we are and what our purpose is in this life.

Keep It Simple

When you first prepare to meditate it is wise not to set yourself great goals. I mean, don't think that by sitting down and listening to soft music and closing your eyes you will find yourself enlightened at the end of it. Nor should you assume that you will be given psychic predictions of the future of the world or taken to high realms of the spirit world. I regret to inform you that that's highly unlikely. But it doesn't matter. Instead, just learn to be still. Learn to bring your body and mind into a harmonious rhythm through your breathing.

Keep it very simple to begin with. Sit in a place where you feel comfortable and won't be distracted. Give yourself enough time – don't be worrying that you only have a few minutes. This type of thinking will only cause you to be stressed – the very opposite of what you want to achieve.

Practising Meditation

Sit in a way that is comfortable to you. So, if you wish to meditate while sitting on a chair, do so, or if you wish to sit on the floor on a cushion, do that – whatever makes you feel relaxed. The only thing I would suggest about sitting is to have your back positioned as straight and upright as your body will allow without straining, and to uncross your legs, because that can impede the flow of blood around your body. This is only important if developing mediumship; in other forms of meditation it is fine

Some people choose to listen to music while they meditate, while others prefer to just sit in the quiet of the place they are in. Again, whatever feels right to you!

To begin with, you are just learning how to sit and breathe and make your body and mind work together. So, your breathing is next. If you have never tried to use breathing exercises before it might feel awkward to begin with, but stay with it, because breathing is the focus of your meditation and the first natural rhythm of the body. Furthermore, normally your mind operates your breathing naturally for you, so when you focus on it, you are taking the controls if you like.

Good breathing is when you inhale through your nose, deep into your lungs in a slow, deliberate motion. Try to fill as much of your lungs with air as you can before slowly and deliberately exhaling. The motion of breathing like this should mean that your body feels as if it is expanding in all directions when you breathe in and contracting and relaxing as you breathe out.

Sometimes, before I began my practice, I would put my hand on my stomach and feel it being pushed forward as I inhaled. And as I exhaled I would gently apply some pressure from my hand to flatten my stomach as the air emptied from my body. This would help me to be aware of the rhythm I was hoping to achieve through my meditation.

Focusing on the breath and motion of the body is all that you need to do at first. You may find that thoughts will enter into your mind during your practice, but try not to clear your mind or make it blank in these early stages. Instead, be aware of them and try not to attach any attention to them. Whenever you experience this type of disturbance, just remind yourself of your breathing pattern.

Also, it would be wise to sit for just a short time to begin with. This way you learn to build up mental strength. Training your mind in meditation is just like training your body in fitness. It would be unwise to try to run a marathon without having started with very short bursts of exercise. So I would suggest 10 to 15 minutes of meditation to start with, and if you can last this long without constantly being distracted or falling asleep, then you can increase the time period. Remember, the worst thing that can happen to you in such an exercise is that you can't concentrate or that you indeed fall asleep.

So now, why not try it? This meditation, from my CD *An Introduction to the Spirit World*, will help you to reconnect to yourself, to that inner voice.

Connecting to your Inner Voice

- First, find a comfortable sitting position. Feel relaxed and calm. Make sure you do not feel restricted by tight or uncomfortable clothing.

- Close your eyes.

- Be aware of your posture. Try, to the best of your ability, to sit with a straight back. Allow your head to sit as straight and steady as possible. If you feel your head fall forward or to the side, try to imagine, if you will, a fine thread connecting to your crown and just tugging you upwards if you feel your head relax and move out of position.

- Now that you've corrected your posture, it is very important that you learn to breathe in an appropriate manner. Breathing in through your nose, taking as much air as you can deep into your lungs, relaxes the body and allows you to feel your first sense of peace.

- Become aware, as you breathe deeply into your body, of your lungs filling up and causing your stomach to swell ... and as you breathe out, let go. Just relax and release the air from your body.

- Start to become aware of your body's natural rhythm as you breathe gently in and out through your nose.

- Feel the natural rhythm and harmony moving the body in and out. This is the first natural harmony of the physical body.

- Use your mind to focus on the air moving in and out through your nose.

- Become fixed on this visualization of the air moving in and out of the body.

- Feel how still you have become.

- Be aware of the weight of your body.

- And be aware that you are visualizing the first separation of mind and body. Your focus is on your breathing and your body is in an automatic state of breathing in its own natural rhythm.

- Visualize, if you will, an abundance of pure white light sitting just above your crown and allow it to pour down through your head, deep down into your body, filling your body with its beautiful white light.

- Become aware of how light your body feels, how bright.

- Let the white light pour through your body in time to the rhythm of your breathing.

- And feel the peace that it brings with it.

- Become aware of how light and subtle you feel, as if you could move upwards, up and away from the body, into the higher part of the mind, the higher part of the mind where you find clarity as you realize that all is well.

- And be at peace with yourself, recognizing that in this state of being you are still, you are peaceful and you are contented.

- Allow yourself to send signals to your body from this higher state of mind, using that quiet inner voice that connects the lower and higher mind together. Send positive signals of peace and contentment to your body.

- Know that in this state of clarity you know no fear and that all the fears which the body has gathered and held can be dispelled in this state of contented mind.

- Send down signals to your body that all is well. And that you are where you should be.

- Be still when all around you is in motion.

- Be calm in the face of all adversities.

- And realize that you can tap into this higher state of being, that it is your right to do so, at any given time.

- Take a little time to enjoy this elevated state of mind.

- Start to allow yourself to feel comfortable in this state of being.

- And just recognize that around your body this beautiful brilliant white light is emanating in all directions.

- Feel it starting to move back towards your body, regenerating and healing old scars, old memories, shining light onto any fears and darknesses held within the body.

- Feel that light come through your body and move now in an upward direction and out through your crown.

- Feel the peace that has moved into your body and feel reconnected to the higher part of yourself that connects you to all things.

- Feel the relaxation that your body has accepted.

- And start to breathe deeply into your lungs, filling them up with air.

- And start to become more aware of the body's natural rhythm of breathing, in and out

- Be aware of the weight of your body as you sit relaxed.

- With each in-breath, become more aware of where your physical being is, reconnecting mind and body to this place and time, telling yourself, 'Coming back, reconnecting...'

- Take nice deep breaths. Draw the oxygen into your body and bring clarity back to your mind, ready to enter back into this waking state of consciousness.

- And come back.

- Open your eyes.

- Breathing deeply, just allow your body to accept the relaxation and peace it's found.

- Now you are ready to face the day.

What I always found when using this practice and teaching it to those who were just beginning their journey was that everyone who did it felt more positive and relaxed at the end of it. I hope that goes for you too!

Take It Easy

Take things easy to begin with. Some people would recommend that you sit in meditation for an hour at first, but it may be that you do not last an hour, and if you have no experience of meditation, why should you be able to? It is worth practising it when you feel moved to do it, but don't overdo it – it isn't that by meditating more you'll develop more quickly. Meditation just gives you a quiet place to go to let things process through your mind. It's the theory, if you like, and the practical work is done in your everyday life. The idea is not to cut yourself off from the world but to become spiritual through living a life in it. So take it slowly – even a few minutes once a day is better than nothing at all. Those ten minutes or so are already an improvement; they are already a step closer to where you want to be and, more importantly, a step closer to improving your mindset and healing any problems and fears you may have.

So, relax. Calm down. Practise how to breathe. With that practice, you will no longer hyperventilate, should you become anxious. Anyone can benefit from this. In fact anyone who doesn't wish to help themselves feel better *deserves* to feel anxious! So sit down. Unwind. Find some calming music, something that's nurturing to your mind, if you feel it will help you. Meditation to heal your psyche does not need to be performed in complete silence in the lotus position! It does not need you to *do*, it just needs you to *be*. To relax, however you feel you can.

As time goes on and you gain more experience, you will naturally shift into a way of meditating that works best for you, but in the meantime, in these initial stages, be kind to yourself. You may fall asleep, but at this early stage that's fine; it only tells you that your mind is not able to sustain you in a relaxed state yet. You may not be able to manage more than a few minutes. That doesn't matter. You may become distracted. That doesn't matter either. Your perseverance matters and your relaxation matters. So continue, however you can. The results will be worth it.

And remembering to allow yourself to *be* rather than *do* will help you throughout your development and indeed your whole life.

Here is a self-healing meditation from my CD *The Healing Power of Mediumship* which will help you to open up your mind to create wellbeing for your body and mind.

Self-Healing

- As with all meditations, find yourself a comfortable place to sit, wearing loose, comfortable clothes.

- Sit with your back in a straight position.

- And start to breathe easily, breathing in through your nose, filling your lungs with air and relaxing your body.

- Follow the breath moving in through your body, allowing your body to rise and fall, all the while becoming more and more relaxed.

- Send out a thought from your mind: 'I am relaxed and I am still. I am at peace and all is well.'

- And as the body relaxes, become more aware of your breathing, of the pattern of your breath moving in and out of your body.

- Focus now on the more subtle energies, the vibrations around your body.

- Try to become aware of the pulse that moves through your body as it becomes stiller and as the subtle energies become much more in focus.

- And tell yourself, 'I am healing my body.'

- And as you do so, visualize a subtle gold energy moving up through your feet, from the earth, moving into your body, all the way up through your legs, into your stomach and up through your torso, filling your body with the wellbeing of the earth energy, moving upwards into your chest...

- Feel this subtle energy healing and calming any tensions, any illness that might be in the body.

- Feel it moving up into the back of your neck, moving up through your head, filling your body completely with the golden energy of the earth.

- Allow this energy to move all through your body, healing old scars and wounds, removing tensions and anxieties, ridding your body of any fear that is trapped in any position.

- And recognize that your body can be healed.

- Allow the golden energy to move up through the crown and out of the body so that it spills over.

- Feel yourself being encompassed by this vital golden energy moving up through the body and moving all through the body as you sit relaxed.

- And visualize for a moment a white light above your crown.

- And ask the higher spirit beings if they will allow you to bring down that white light to heal your mind. (They will always allow you to do so, but it is only courteous to ask.)

- See the light spiralling downwards, above your head, down over your shoulders, passing down through your arms and your body, all the way down your legs, right down to your feet.

- Feel this white light spiralling over you.

- Allow this clear pure spirit energy to release any memories of fear, to release any tensions that have held you back in this life.

- And recognize that in this state of mind you can heal your mind.

- And tell yourself, 'I am well ... and all is well in my life.'

- At this higher state of mind you can see fears and problems in your everyday life for what they are, as you recognize that you are spirit and you are much greater than these fears and problems.

- Feel all the old fears being washed away by this white light spiralling down over your body, cleansing your mind, casting light into any dark rooms in your mind.

- Visualize, if you will, the golden light moving up from the earth through your body and the white light spiralling down, cleansing and clearing all past illness.

- And allow yourself to sit still in this visualization.

- And start to breathe, as you watch the white light moving slowly in a clockwise direction back up off the body, all the way up, and the gold light spiralling back down all the way through your body back towards the earth.

- Breathe nice and deeply now as you come back to waking consciousness.

- With each breath, recognize that you are sitting in your room, relaxed and comfortable, and that you are becoming more and more aware, more focused on the here and now.

- Breathing in, relaxing, breathing out, releasing, and feeling good. Coming back...

- Until you are fully awake and in the room.

Excitement and Anticipation

Looking back, I often wish the entire journey to spiritual development could be as simple as the early stages. At the outset I remember being filled with excitement, anticipation and a tremendous eagerness to learn. At that point the undiscovered country that is your own mind is totally open to being charted, ready for a journey into your soul – a journey that could be as vast as the universe itself or as small as a grain of sand. Who knows? Interest is high, your heart is filled with passion and your head is bursting, keen with interest. I remember it so well – all systems are *go*!

Then, without warning, and completely against your instincts, you are instructed to meditate. Get quiet. Be patient. Go slowly, slowly, and calm the inner self. *Not* what the eager new student wants to hear, or do! Yet with the benefit of hindsight, I have to agree. The first and perhaps most crucial lesson in spiritual development is learning to sit and listen and be calm.

You know already that you can do this by yourself, and with hard work and dedication you may be able to open up to spirit on your own, though it is definitely best to devote your energies to finding a group. Once in a group you will find that it is not just a place to develop your experience of the world around you; it can, and almost always does, involve developing your experience of yourself. Surrounded by other people's opinions and ideas and work, you will encounter aspects of yourself that you may never have known existed and you will need to examine any aspect of yourself that you are uncomfortable with. If you do not, they will become a stumbling block when it comes to opening and connecting with spirit, for there are no secrets with spirit. When you develop mediumship, you transform yourself.

And the best way to do this is with a group.

2
The Development Circle

*'When going through development,
you can never go slowly enough.'*
JEAN PRIMROSE

The better your choice of development home, the better progress you are likely to make. So speak to people involved in the churches and ask any heartfelt questions that you may have before you begin.

It is important that you feel good about the people and about the place where you will sit. I know it took me a good deal of sitting in the particular group I chose before I felt totally relaxed. Remember, there will be many barriers to come down, both from within yourself and from the others sitting around you.

Types of Circle

In most Spiritualist groups and circles the developing mediums are furthering their own awareness, allowing their senses to explore the atmosphere around them and thus opening up a whole new set of experiences and gaining a new understanding of the spiritual world.

There are also many circles these days which offer ways to practise psychic readings and undertake clairvoyant practices. 'Clairvoyance' simply means 'to see clearly'. In the case of a psychic it would mean that the psychic reader has a clear vision to offer their sitter. Or, in the case of a medium, clairvoyance would describe how the medium sees the spirit person who is communicating, either via a clear picture in their mind or in some cases objectively standing in front of them.

Another word common to mediums is 'clairaudience'. This is where the medium hears the voice of the spirit and repeats what they are hearing to their sitter. Joan of Arc was said to be clairaudient because she heard the voices of St Catherine and other saints who gave her guidance in her life.

There is another sense which mediums can develop, and that is clairsentience. This simply means 'to sense clearly', i.e. having the feeling of a spirit person close to you and being able to distinguish, for example, what height they were, how they lived or even how they died. Clairsentience is something I believe we all have. Some people get a sense of danger, for instance, or a sense of anticipation before something actually happens. Many psychics are clairsentient and get strong feelings about future events, but mediums who develop this sense in a much deeper way will sense the life of the spirit who is communicating through them.

Sitting in a circle to develop clairvoyance, clairaudience or clairsentience be useful in developing mediumship, but I would always advise people to try to sit in a circle which helps them to develop some form of deeper meditative practice first. This is simply because the value of learning about your own life's journey will help much more when it comes time for you to try and help others with your gift. Empathy plays a very big part in mediumship. When we understand our own life and learn to accept and deal with it, then we can help people in a much deeper way as a medium, because we will have some understanding of their feelings rather than just be offering them answers.

Observation

When you actually find yourself sitting in a development circle, it is important to observe the other people and try to gain some understanding of where they are coming from. Don't be too keen to prove to everyone in the group that you have psychic abilities in order to be accepted. Remember, they have all been where you are, so this is a good opportunity to learn from them.

If, like me, you go into a circle which has already been running for some time and you are the new person there, then it is even more important to be the observer. Don't be in a rush to impress people. Such eagerness might upset the harmony of the group, who will have already formed a bond, and you may end up being resented by the others. I have known many people who were invited into an established circle and disrupted it by their eagerness to impress. Sadly, this either led to them leaving the group, feeling that they were not part of it and complaining that they had not been made welcome, or to them staying in the group but behaving in a very childish manner and constantly looking for attention.

I was lucky that the leader of my first circle, Mrs Primrose, was a seasoned professional. She was in her late seventies when I first met her and had been running circles for years. She told me that I should sit and try to take in what was going on before really tuning in myself. In my early circle days it took me quite some time just to sit still and meditate, let alone try to link to the spirit world or give messages.

Learning about Yourself

The circle is your classroom, where you will be learning about the spirit world, spirit guides and all sorts of altered states and spiritual practices, and, most importantly, about yourself.

Being Honest with Yourself

Becoming a medium means that you have to be totally honest with yourself. How can you possibly help another if you can't help yourself? So recognizing your own emotional baggage and learning to work through it is a very important part of your development.

Ironically, we are often the last person to see who we really are. On the journey to becoming a medium, we will have many opportunities to reflect on how our experiences have changed us as a person. However, there may be parts of ourselves that we are not even aware of but others can see and point out. And this is why group work is important: your group, however large or small, will act as a mirror. Often a character flaw you witness in others and fail to understand or that you become irritated by will be a reflection of your own nature. This in turn will provide many opportunities to examine yourself as well as others. So there is not just a deepening of contact with spirit in a development circle, there is also a deepening of contact with yourself.

If you feel uncomfortable with this, then it is likely that you are not quite ready to move deeper in your spiritual development. That's fine – it's not a bad thing. It's just that you still have some way to go first. Simply focus on relaxing and healing yourself. Work more in meditation and don't be afraid to talk about any obstacles you're facing with other members of the group. Accept whatever help you need, knowing that when you are ready to start your development, spirit will be waiting, patiently and with love.

Relaxing Body and Mind

If you do feel that you are able to go on with your development right now, then it's good to look at the emotional scars from your life and accept them. Guess what? You can do this through meditation.

Relaxing the body in meditation may seem an easy first step here. However, meditation is not about simply relaxing the body – it is also about relaxing the mind, which will take time. When the body is relaxed, the mind tends to become more active! Learning to still your mind can be difficult, especially for those just starting.

A common mistake is that when walking into a development class and relaxing, you think you're relaxed. However, this is not the case at all. Relaxing is letting go of something. It's often letting go of tension. In this case, particularly when starting out, it's letting go of ideas and of habits. This cannot happen in one night; it will more than likely take a couple of years. This is why you need to be very patient, especially in the beginning, and to be gentle with yourself. But other things are happening – you're meeting other people who share your thinking, which also gives you a chance to develop new friendships and experiences. Never think that nothing is happening in development.

Emptying Out the Mind

Working on any mind level through meditation will at some point bring some of your inner thoughts to the surface – a bit like when you have a very vivid dream which seems to have a particular relevance to your life yet makes you feel uneasy because it is not totally familiar to you. I know that I often experienced episodes in my early meditations which would show visually in my mind and make me feel uneasy, but as I grew it became easier to understand that such visions were not coming from the spirit world or guides but from my inner self. It is as if when we relax as in sleep or certain levels of meditation, our psyche relaxes and lets some of our fears or anxieties come to the surface of our mind in symbolic fashion so that we might deal with them and eventually learn from them.

When in meditation like this, you may also encounter psychic phenomena: psychic flashes, precognition, perhaps the emotional states of others around you. Let them pass. It is very easy to get caught up in these, and in some ways they are useful. They tell you that your psychic ability is up and running. However, developing mediumship encompasses far more than just these flashes. While these experiences are demonstrations of talent, this talent still needs to be trained. A good example to illustrate this is that someone may have a flair for cooking and know how to mix ingredients together, but you wouldn't let them serve a banquet.

In any case, I would say that in the first year of your development 90 per cent of what you are experiencing in your meditative state is coming from your deeper self. This happens gradually over time to clear space in the mind. It's a bit like having a cupboard in your home where you throw everything that you don't have use for at the present time, and every now and then you feel an urge to go in there and clear some of the stuff from the past away.

Similarly, at this stage, our mind is emptying out in order to clear space for new knowledge. Such a clearing of the mind will also help you to process your own life at an emotional level. You need to make yourself emotionally and psychologically robust for what is to come later in your development.

Overcoming Fear

Part of this clearing of the mind involves facing up to your fears and overcoming them.

Fear is why many people enter development in the first place. It's often the biggest factor that drives them to attend courses or circles or meditation centres: because they wish to learn why they are scared and how not to be scared. They may actually be unaware of it at the start, but the number of people who come into circles and confess that they are scared is quite high. They may say, 'I'm frightened because it feels as if spirits are coming to get me,' or 'I'm frightened of death.' So, if you are scared, you will find many like-minded people wherever you choose to work!

First of all, you need to recognize what you're frightened of, to recognize what's been holding you back in life. As human beings we have many fears, but the ultimate fear is death – either our own or of that of someone we love. This was one of the fears that I lost in developing mediumship. I realized there was simply no point to it. We're all going to die and there's nothing we can do about it. So there's some good news to start with!

But you cannot die for the life of you – you really cannot.

Through the development that I've done, I've reached a point where I don't believe in life after death, I *know* it. Belief implies some kind of doubt. All my experiences have taken me beyond that. When you reach this point a kind of self-confidence comes into you, because you know there's more to you than the here and now, than the person you are at the moment, that you're part of a much greater stream of life.

I'd like to help you gain the same assurance – to be confident that there is more to life than this – and to leave your fears behind.

Putting on the Light in the Dark Room

There is really nothing to fear but fear itself. But if you have lots of fears and you start out on spiritual development, they can manifest as spirits and hauntings and monsters. If you can overcome your fear, if you can put a light on in the dark rooms of your mind – which is where all the monsters are really coming from – then you'll be fine.

Spirit is infinitely gentle, a very loving, guiding presence. So, don't feel afraid or nervous. You won't encounter anything that you as a person cannot handle, and anything that appears to be negative will always be due to fear on the earth plane. Fear on the spirit plane simply does not exist.

Any fears that you encounter are usually your own. That's why you must learn about them, and learn about yourself. Then you can overcome them. Knowledge – of yourself more than anything else – really is power.

Facing your Fears

For most people, their thoughts are suppressed, often from fear, and this comes out in little ways: panicky moments, bad dreams, insomnia and so on. A lot of these fear-based actions and experiences are because the mind and body are unsettled.

So we must face our fears, including mentally, if we are to develop to the fullest we can. By learning to relax, surrounded by people we can trust and who are all going or have already gone through similar experiences, we can form a healthy mind–body connection – and so a connection with spirit that is healthy.

You don't have to have conquered every doubt and fear to develop mediumship. We are physical and human, and there will always be uncertainties. It's controlling their influence that is key to our progress.

With this in mind, I feel I must say that becoming a medium does not fix someone; that is entirely up to them. It is a reason and an incentive to change yourself, but it is not a solution. You yourself must find the way to overcome your fears and uncertainties.

Do not be discouraged by this, or be afraid if you feel it is a challenge. It is more than possible, especially if you take it slowly. Many people do not even notice how and when they change!

You will know when you have changed, though, because your life circumstances will change. What meditation will do – what working and encountering spirit will do – is prepare you for bigger situations in the future. A possibility that would most likely have terrified you at a younger age – a death in the family, for example – will become much more acceptable to you in the future.

Secrets

Another thing to bear in mind is that secrets are not good things in development: they create tension, and will slip out if not processed correctly. If you are carrying things that have happened and you don't feel quite ready to share them, try and process them as best as you can, either alone or with professional help such as counselling. You can do this either before entering development or at the same time.

Before you even consider going into any spiritual class, you must bear in mind that when you start participating in a class, your emotional life may be opened up to you. When it's a spiritual development group, though, essentially those in spirit are in control and they are caring. So it will not be an immediate, sudden opening: it will be gentle, and with great love, at the pace you can handle.

Working in a Group
All Kinds of People

Something else to remember in development circles is that you will encounter people from all walks of life, and you may not 'click' with every member of the circle, especially if you have joined an open circle. It is likely that there will be some whose personalities will rub against yours. Try to remember at all times that all of you have a shared goal – you are all in the same boat, if you like – which will help to smooth out any problems you may encounter.

I know what this is like, because I used to get really annoyed by a few individuals in my circle. I saw aspects and personality traits that irritated me: someone would be really impatient, while someone else would endlessly complain. One or two even insisted they were feeling other circle members' pain!

I wondered for years why they acted in the way they did. Why did this person keep saying they could only feel pain? Why did that person never seem happy? Didn't they realize that they were bringing bad energy to circle? Then suddenly my mindset changed and instead I started wondering why their traits irritated me. It took me a long time to realize that I was actually annoyed at my *own* traits that I saw reflected in others. *They* weren't 'bringing bad energy' – *I* was, through being negative about them. I couldn't change them – and indeed I shouldn't – but I could, and did, change what I disliked about myself.

This was a valuable lesson for whenever I was frustrated by the actions of others: they were acting in their way, and I was reacting in mine.

This reflection and examination of self is vital to gaining an eventual understanding of spirit. Shifting your mindset to foster empathy and an understanding of others will build a compassion that is vital to any successful spiritual working. We are all connected by spirit and to spirit. Our emotional links are what enable us to form contact with loved ones who have crossed. Mediumship is not just about connecting through this link, it is about understanding it in order to translate the information we receive from spirit in as clear and as healthy a way as possible.

Another reason for understanding rather than fighting with others is that the struggle will only impede your own progress. By fighting and feeling tense, you simply cannot relax, which is the key for connecting with spirit. You are not open, so contact simply cannot be made.

So, if you do feel negative about some people in your circle, examine why as soon as possible. Ask yourself, 'If I'm annoyed by that, can *I* be like that, and if so, where?' The answers may surprise you, but whatever they may be, they will help you, and so help others.

Children in the Circle

Without being patronizing, I see members of any circle, especially those just starting, as children. Like children we are eager to learn what our spirit 'parent' has to show us! And we can also have some very childish habits that need to be examined and, if necessary, corrected.

To start with, there are those 'children' who always want attention and may overact in order to get that. This is common with those who tend to gush in circle: they often become over-emotional and appear weak and needy.

In my development, there was a 'needy child' of the type I have just mentioned. We'll call him Mr Witter. He would stand up and talk for longer than everyone else, and when he spoke, it was often without any meaning. It reminded me of a child trying to tell his mother something, and it deeply frustrated me at times. However, it made me realize that although I thought I was a patient person, I actually had very little tolerance. It helped me to improve myself. Interestingly, when I learned to relax when Mr Witter was wittering on, he calmed down as well. My choice to act in a different way made both of us better people.

There is a Mr Witter in every circle – someone who takes up time and rarely gives coherent, meaningful messages. They want more attention and energy than anyone else and can seem draining.

There are other types of people in circle, too. Another is a member who seeks attention in another sense – the 'poor me', who at the end of each session will tell a tale of woe to gain pity. They may say, 'Whilst I was sitting, the spirits came and now I feel ill. I feel weak. It took a lot out of me.' Or they may say, 'I sit here and help everyone. I could feel *your* pain tonight.'

What is actually the case if that they're not feeling anyone else's pain. They're actually opening up themselves and so experiencing their own; they then try to translate it into something that they can understand. I personally understood 'poor me' a lot more quickly than the 'needy child': I realized that these were the ones who needed to be healed and were, indirectly at least, asking for healing.

Then there is the excitable child, who never gets much out of meditating in circle: they simply want to stand up and be noticed. An excitable child is the one that, all through meditation, rather than being still, will be thinking about what to say to the group!

On reflection, I think *I* was the excitable child! I wanted to be accepted, so I made a friendly noise. I had a real need to please and tell people the right things and make them happy. It took a while before I realized that I didn't need to make people happy or make an effort to be accepted – people would accept me for who I was.

With an open group there are people of all different levels and abilities, so I was able to notice very early on that I did my best when I *wasn't* the excitable child, when I kept quiet and learned to just be. It was when I started to compete and play and get attention that it became difficult for me. So often what you don't realize is that you've made it difficult for yourself – and for others too.

Then there is the spoiled child, who may wait right until the end of the night and then mysteriously 'receive a message' just as everyone has finished. Sometimes this does happen, but for the spoiled child, it happens every time. They will even pretend to be under spirit control or in a trance to get attention, and appear uncomfortable because everyone else is at peace.

There are many other types, but these are the most common. Which child are you taking to development tonight? If you can recognize inappropriate behaviour, you can correct it before it becomes a habit and so much more difficult to change.

The Inner Child

It may come as a surprise to witness and display childish behaviour. Why would it appear in circle, when surrounded by adults and by everyone earnest and eager to learn about spirit? It's because in a good circle there is a good teacher, and psychologically that teacher becomes an authority figure. So it becomes like a parent/child relationship.

Ultimately, you will need to transform this relationship into one of psychological equals. It does no good to think you are less or more than others, regardless of experience, and if you don't see that your inner child exists, and needs to be understood as much as everyone else's, it will be very difficult to let go of it.

Fighting with others like a child is the biggest drawback you can have in development. By fighting rather than simply being still, you demonstrate that you are no better than them. Often spirit will view this and see you are not ready to accept what they may give you. You may receive details that you personally find troubling over the course of your life as a medium, and it is important that you do not react emotionally to them. You are not in a place to judge anyone's actions: you are here to communicate and to heal, always with love.

Understanding and Compassion

Understanding and compassion are very different: you can understand someone, but compassion is a conscious decision to use that understanding to be a better person. For example, I decided after a while that instead of observing and getting frustrated by Mr Witter, I would befriend him and understand why he was acting the way he was and work out a way of getting what he needed – which turned out to be simply a friend in the group.

Keeping this knowledge in mind, especially if you are just starting to develop, will help you if you find other people in circle troublesome. I believe it is much fairer to warn you of any potential troubles you may find as you work spiritually in a physical world rather than focus entirely on the spiritual aspect of developing mediumistic ability. Developing understanding and compassion is in itself part of developing mediumship: a good medium will be able to see past someone's childish reactions and, more importantly, refuse to get drawn into them. Rather they will see that everyone has a higher nature and that people are often expressing their fears, rather than spirit.

Compassion does not just lie in offering tea and a biscuit! True compassion lies in forgiveness: forgiving our trespasses, as we forgive those who trespass against us.

The Teacher

Some members of a circle will actually fall out with the teacher, sometimes right from the very beginning. They challenge them with statements like, 'You don't know as much as you're telling us.' There are those who are wilful as well and who want to take over the group, because they are used to taking over in every other aspect of their lives. They will gain confidence – but not necessarily knowledge or aptitude. This can fool the group, and other members can even be weakened by it, wondering whether to follow the wilful child or the teacher.

A good teacher must be able to guide the group when necessary, but not be domineering, and to deal with everybody in the group with patience and skill. As a member of a circle, you should gain confidence from the strength of that teacher, which should be of a compassionate kind. Overall, though, they must be able to control. They should be grounded, not floaty and flighty. If you are surrounded by people firing off messages in all directions, and even starting arguments, you will need someone with the experience and right nature to bring everything – and everyone – to order.

Sometimes people blame their teacher for their lack of progress: 'I'm not getting anywhere! They're not good enough!' If you really feel that way, then there's an easy answer: find another teacher. You are not obliged to stay in a circle.

I actually get a lot of people coming up to me and saying, 'I hate my circle.' My first thought about this is, 'If you hate your circle, why? Is it something to do with you, or is it because you have a bad teacher or a bad group? Why don't you fit there? Is there anything you can do to stay and make the group better with your presence and your energy?'

Open Circles

The fact that an open circle is just that – open to all – can further unsettle members. There is no specific format such as you would get with a smaller, closed circle. However, there is a clear reason why an open circle formed by a Spiritualist church or organization can get so many members: with so many people, there is a wide scope for opportunity. Every week it changes and there are no regular sitters – someone may only be there for two weeks and never come back.

Above all, in an open circle, you have to learn not to become affected by all of what you witness: with so many members, there are also a lot of people to share your energy with. It will take time for you to form links. But as a place that offered lessons, I found an open circle to be excellent, because I found I had to dig deeper. So stick with it, if you find it difficult. You may be surprised at what you gain from persevering!

Give Yourself Time

When you make the decision to start out in a Spiritualist circle, try not to enter that group with your psychic energies bursting out all over the place, expecting things to happen at once. Give yourself plenty of time – time to adjust to the other sitters and time to get used to the collective energy of the group. Give yourself the chance to learn to sit in meditation quietly and to acclimatize yourself to your new surroundings, remembering that the two most important of the five human senses you have at this moment are sight and hearing. Use them. Listen and observe. Hear and watch. And above all, try not to be overly enthusiastic.

One of the biggest misconceptions about developing mediumship is that it can happen quickly. The truth is that nothing is set in stone, except that developing mediumship takes time. *Lots* of time in some cases. So please let go of any thoughts of becoming a medium overnight. It simply does not happen. We need to discover our own mental processes and to trust in ourselves and others. We need to relax. We need to tame our ego.

We are all taught by spirit teachers who are patient, deliberate and careful as to how they bring us along. More about them later, but be prepared to invest time and energy with your teachers and remember that spiritual development, unlike Polaroid film, does *not* develop immediately! So relax, make the most of the peaceful setting of your circle and surrender yourself to the process.

I must stress again that you are not expected to *try*; you are simply expected to *be*. When you try, when you push instead of allowing yourself to relax, you become the child that has to prove itself. The part of you that needs to compete has taken over. *It will not help you!* Just relax and be.

Persevere...

It is easy to feel nervous when you first develop your mediumship. After all, you will be letting down your guard around people you will not know that well at first and showing a level of emotion that you may not be used to displaying. If you continue to find it uncomfortable, remember, there's no shame in walking away from one group and finding another. With circles, you have to be able to trust the people you are with, and if you don't, it's not the right circle for you. However, I would advise you to do your best to establish why a group is not right for you, and see whether this can be righted, before you make that decision.

A good example of persevering will come through when you do progress to working with a smaller circle, with no one but people you trust and who trust you. Then it becomes easier, not least because there are fewer people to compete with! Surprised by this? You may very well find, as you encounter more about spirit and in spirit, that you suddenly want to be the best. Competition to an extent is healthy for self-reflection and to help us improve, but it is very easy for some members to let it take over and divert them from their real purpose: to learn and experience spirit. Learning about this and similar aspects of your personality as soon as you can, and taming them all so that you control them rather than they control you, will help you progress as a whole much more easily – and often more quickly as well.

I went into a large development circle myself and found it offered the best range of experience for me. I encountered many different types of people, some I got on with better than others, but it was the only circle I knew of and so the only one I could be in at the time. Being in a large circle meant I could form friendships with a few people, which in turn helped me weather any clashes of personality that I had. I found a core of people in the much larger circle, about six of us from about 40 in total, where the energy seemed to flow better and continued to do so as time went on. Later on, we formed our own private circle.

Pacing Yourself

Whatever sort of group you are in, remember that the whole aim of spirit is to learn to share, not to compete, not to say, 'Look at me!' Ask yourself how you can stop competing with someone who learns faster than you and how you can learn to work in a way that's right for you. The pace that is best for someone else is often not suitable for you at all.

Also remember that other members of your circle will have ways of contacting spirit that you won't, and vice versa. It is possible to have circles devoted to specific purposes – trance circles, for example – but building a circle without enough experience of spirit or enough knowledge of yourself can pose a problem. In any circle it takes time to establish the members' roles and mutual trust. Trance circles take much longer to establish, primarily because of any fears that members bring in. You must be sure of yourself mentally and emotionally to sit in such a circle, and this is rare when you take the first few steps into developing mediumship.

I will give you a very good example of why it is best to find your own pace and level, and also why it is important to learn compassion, no matter what pace you progress at. Many years after I left my open circle, I was asked by a young man about how to develop as a medium. After giving him some of the advice you'll find in this book, I suggested that he go to his local open circle, which happened to be my old one, and see how he felt. He said, 'I have. But there's this man and he's really putting me off.' I had to ask who it was, and was very surprised to find out it was in fact Mr Witter! For him, the open circle had become a place to go and keep similar company and to talk about his interests rather than develop.

I found out that in the early days he simply would not be told the best way to develop; he refused and stayed where he was. I believe it is a shame when someone cannot or does not choose to progress. However, Mr Witter, and others like him, are well worth remembering when we question why we need compassion, what our reasons are behind developing ourselves, and how we need to pace ourselves.

It's what you want to put into the practice, and what you want to do for others, that will become the main factors in your progress; the best teacher in the world cannot guide someone who is unwilling to learn.

It may be hard for you to be around difficult people, but helping our fellow man is exactly what developing mediumship is about. Only you know how long or short a time this will take you. And be kind to yourself and to others – you are all overcoming a lifetime of conditioning. It will take time.

For me, settling into my circle took some six months or so. Each of us was at a different stage of development, so I tried very hard to just stay focused on what was unfolding and evolving for me.

Healing in the Group

The healing of negative experiences or thought patterns helps the group as a whole by giving all members hope and understanding.

For example, in one circle, there was a lady who during her meditations repeatedly encountered her spirit guide, a woman who said she had been raped. Each week the story would progress. Several years later, it emerged that she herself had been raped as a little girl, and what she had experienced during her meditation had reflected her own experiences exactly. The process greatly helped her to heal – it offered a powerful therapy for her.

If you are or become a teacher of a group, you need to recognize the difference between spiritual experience and cleansing experience, and remember spirit would not show someone inexperienced something so negative.

This also explains bad dreams: when people enter a deep sleep, a truly relaxed sleep, often it allows the subconscious levels of the mind to surface and process negative events and possibilities, transforming thinking patterns into something beneficial rather than destructive. And often bad or sad memories rise to the surface to be dealt with. So when you're relaxed in a meditating group – not just physically relaxed, but *mentally* relaxed – your mental processes will be much as they are in deep sleep. And you will be transforming yourself.

Ongoing Development

I still sit in a development circle with a few people that I have formed extremely close links with over the years. The decision to develop is truly a lifelong one. You can never say that you know everything there is to know. So development is ongoing, as is working through bad habits. Sometimes we can pick them up as we change, but it's more an ongoing process where you continuously refine yourself. There are still things I have to work on.

Often the reason why I still have behaviour that I haven't changed or shaped in a way that makes it acceptable to me is that I haven't encountered a situation where that behaviour would need to emerge. But, thanks to my work in development, I know that if I do encounter a new situation, especially one that is unpleasant, I will find it a lot easier to accept, thanks to my work both with spirit and as a medium.

It is helpful to realize that you can react to situations in a way that helps or hinders. Developing yourself in a circle, and gaining experience of yourself, others and spirit, will combine to put you in very good stead, whatever you may face. This experience, and the knowledge that you can choose how to react and behave, strengthen as much as they humanize. With mediumship, you do not just develop skills that help others, you develop skills that help yourself.

For example, I used to take responsibility for the 'what ifs' – I used to think it would be my fault if something happened to my two young sons. However, as I stayed in development and grew, I realized that I personally had no control over life or death – I had only my own personal reaction towards events as large as these.

There will always be scope to improve yourself, though I would say that as you grow spiritually, other facets of your work will become more important than self-improvement. However, it is always wise to go back and re-examine your psyche from time to time and ask yourself if it has projected any aspect of yourself onto the messages you give. You must always be aware of how much of any message is from yourself and how much is from spirit. Over time, as you practise and gain greater awareness, spirit will come through more, but with you as a channel there is likely to be some residual part of you that comes through as well, especially in the beginning. The better you become, the less this happens.

Developing Character

Ultimately, sitting in a circle is not just about developing mediumship, it is about developing *character*. It's about bolstering yourself as a person, realizing your weaknesses and transforming them into strengths. In that sense, you are processing your mind and turning it into a more psychologically robust place to work from.

So there is much more to development than learning to be a healer or a medium – it is about building the inner strength to face life. No matter where your spiritual journey takes you, the result of development, for almost everybody, is a shaping and building of character.

It's a natural gravitation, to want to shift from fear to something that is above that fear. But the ultimate is to find a balance between this life and the next. At this stage, knowing they both exist and can be bridged is enough: do not be in a rush to head to either. Rather just enjoy the experience of being in between, knowing you can communicate with both. The development circle is often the ideal place to experience this 'in-between' stage.

Tips for Development in a Circle

- Be eager to go to your circle but not over-eager when you sit.

- Be very patient and don't always expect spiritual experiences to occur just because you are sitting quietly, listening to soft music and meditating.

- Try to always attend and treat what you do in your circle with great respect. The more you dedicate yourself to the circle, the more you will gain from it.

- Don't carry it home with you or let it encroach on your everyday life. What happens in the circle stays in the circle.

- Try to remain grounded in your everyday life. It is good to let the mind rest from all things spiritual – after all, you would have to rest your body after physical exercise. The same applies when you exercise your mind.

3
Linking with Spirit

*'The teachings of the spirit are learned through
the experience, not just the words.'*
A MALE GUIDE SPEAKING THROUGH A WOMAN CALLED
LAURA WHO WAS PART OF MY EARLY CIRCLE

Embarrassing as it seems, for the best part of my first six
months in circle, I often fell asleep! I couldn't seem to
meditate for asking all sorts of questions of myself, none of
which I could answer. All of my past spiritual experiences
suddenly seemed so distant and faded; I couldn't even be
sure if they had really occurred. It often seemed as if *nothing
at all* was happening.

Or so I thought, anyway. I have since learned that there
is always a part of you growing, even if you don't recognize
it at the time and even if it happens while you sleep. Every
now and again there would be some sort of semi-spiritual
experience for me – you know, the 'I thought I saw a spirit
person' kind of thing or the 'I think I felt someone touch
me' sort of sensation. Then, when I listened to the accounts

of all the other sitters in the group, I would feel that my little experiences were nothing much, maybe even figments of my imagination or conjured up out of my desire, so I would become despondent.

Watching the Mind Traffic

Then, as time passed on, I found the next obstacle to understand and overcome was an endless stream of visual images and thoughts racing through my mind that did not seem to belong to me, often accompanied by conditions of what felt like real physical pain. From time to time I even had sensations of floating outside my own body.

It would be easy for any new student to explain away these happenings as paranormal events activated by some higher spiritual beings outside one's own self. But from where? By whom? And how? More often than not, it is actually the mind of the newly developing medium beginning to expand and open up, exploring some of the archives of their own subconscious.

Looking back to those early development days now with much clearer understanding, I definitely feel that most of those experiences were, in fact, the clearing out of my own mental garbage – a myriad of thoughts and feelings that lay buried beneath the uppermost layer of my consciousness. Tempting as it is to explain every event that happens in circle as spirit-related, much that happens at first is really a clearing-out process.

With increased practice of relaxation methods, the upper conscious mind will begin to relax, giving way to what has been stored in the deeper sub-levels of the mind, allowing stored memories to come up and float to the surface. This is not too dissimilar to the kinds of dreams you might experience when your mind is close to waking – vivid pictures and feelings, which at first do not appear to relate to your own life, begin to take shape and form in your mind's eye. As you grow in awareness, you will learn how to distinguish what is relevant to you on your journey and what can be left behind.

But it is only once you have truly encountered spiritual phenomena for the first time that you can begin to place things in their proper context and distinguish between the internal and the external mind traffic.

Write It All Down

It is wise to keep a diary of all mental activity that occurs for you as you move further and further along your development path. A bit like recording your dreams, write the details down, however trivial they may appear to you to be at the time. Some interesting or enlightening patterns may emerge in due course, providing you with valuable insights. And there is no better fail-safe than dated documentation, even if only for your own records and satisfaction.

Your diary will become a valuable tool charting your progress on your mind's journey. After all, as the first stage of development is all about clearing out the vaults of your mind so that the higher spirit can find a place to link with you, what better way to make room than by capturing it all elsewhere on paper?

Recognize your own Spirit

Another very important consideration as you embark on this path is being in touch with your own physical well-being and personal energy field. Remember, as you prepare to link with a higher energy, spirit energy, your body must be ready for the heightened flow. In order for you to house such a force, let alone try to comprehend it at such an early stage, you must first begin to recognize the closest field of energy to you – in other words, *your own spirit*. There is absolutely no point in trying to find out about other spirit guides or the gifts of spirit until you embrace the realization that *you* yourself are a spirit!

Be Patient

Forming a link with spirit takes years and so often people get impatient. 'Why won't they come to me?' 'Why won't they give me anything?' It's not that they don't want to, it's that you're not ready for it. It helps to listen to what you're actually saying. If you're blaming others for not giving you things, that shows you something about yourself. Constantly blaming others will be holding you back.

So if you're feeling upset because you're not being 'given' anything, turn it round and think in terms of not being ready to receive what's out there waiting for you. That change of attitude in itself should help you along in your development. And when you're ready to receive, you will.

Meeting Spirit

Experiencing spirit for the first time is different for everyone, but no matter how they describe it — 'I felt this rush,' 'I felt something drop' — people are aware that something 'otherly' happens. Often they will state that they saw something, but sadly it turns out to be just in their mind. The key is not to see but to *feel* spirit. With mediumship, it's not about seeing, it's *feeling* that's believing.

My first experience of completely linking with spirit, rather than just touching the boundaries as I had before, made every experience before pale into insignificance. I couldn't even start to compare the slight brushes of spirit to the genuine connection that I experienced then. It is extremely difficult to describe the upliftment that linking gave me; the scope of spirit is extremely hard to limit in words. For the first time in my life I no longer believed – it surpassed my faith. I could *feel* spirit: its immensity, and knowledge, and above all love. The reality of it blew my mind and was among the most important experiences of my life.

Until then I had been frustrated that while I was seeing and hearing things and could even give messages and act as a bridge to spirit, I could not cross that bridge to stand in spirit's lands. In all honesty I believe the final leap to make that connection, though I cannot describe how, was made possible through my sheer frustration. I was starting to doubt, saying, 'If something doesn't change, if I don't feel this as a sense of reality, *is* it real? I don't need to just *believe* – I need to *know*.' And, then, suddenly, I had connected to that higher realm. I knew what spirit felt like. It was like learning to ride a bicycle – one moment I was frustrated and then, suddenly, I had it. I had the knack, and I knew I would never forget it.

It could still be that it was a part of my higher mind that I saw as separate in order to learn from it. But whatever aspect was shown to me, whether it was my higher self or those that are fully of spirit, it was the most wonderful feeling I have ever encountered. I choose to see that it was a glimpse of what it was like to be spirit rather than a spiritual being on a physical journey.

Is It Spirit?

With that experience, I realized that you need to understand something deeper – to understand how *real* spirit is – to really develop as a medium.

Many people come onto this path and get stuck because they are very unsure. They often ask, 'Was it me or was it spirit? Is what's happening to me really happening or am I imagining it? Am I making all of this up?'

The ability to distinguish between what is internal and what is being shown to you from spirit is a most important area of development for the potential working medium. At this point those of you who do not wish to continue developing in this particular direction will become drawn much more to the psychic levels of your own consciousness, seeing distant visions and picking up conditions close to you, mostly all on a very material plane.

You may experience physical situations while communicating with spirit too, but the best way to find out if something *is* spirit or your mind is to see if it is repeated.

The Earliest Psychic Level

When trying to link with spirit, look out for the same set of sensations happening each time you sit. For me it was a feeling of having a fine wispy beard, wearing a robe type of garment and my hands moving slowly but spontaneously, as if performing some sort of *tai chi*.

At first I wondered what in the world was happening to me. When I asked Mrs Primrose, she told me to be patient and to ask the spirit world. She said that when I was ready to know, they would tell me.

After some time I began to ignore these events, because my mind was more interested in getting messages for other sitters. I was becoming stuck at the earliest psychic level. Instead of registering the impressions of the spirits who were trying to link with me, I chose to ignore them in order to read from the psychic data banks.

Some people, of course, will be content to remain at this stage. Some mediums working only at the level of this energy field can bring through marvellous evidence and also often gain an understanding of the psychic field, somewhat like psychometrists, who can read a person's life history from a particular object, or psychic healers, who are able to pinpoint an illness or make a proper diagnosis just by touching a patient. Psychic experiences can be colourful and fantastic and quite distracting. But the student who wishes to investigate mediumship to the full must go deeper within and not allow themselves to be content with this first stage.

I remember myself being easily distracted at this early level, thinking I had discovered the key to being a good medium, but something deeper inside me welled up, driving me on. I wanted to know more about the limitless source and incredible force behind the power of spirit, so I persevered. I suggest you do the same.

What's Happening for *You*?

Sitting in meditation, resting in the calmness and the stillness, I found myself becoming more at peace with myself. Even so, I still asked questions in my mind. I was so eager to find out about my possible spirit guides and what type of spiritual work I might be able to do. And what about the 'gifts' of the spirit I had heard mentioned by other mediums? What were mine to be? And when would I get to start putting them to good use?

The early days of development can be very trying, especially when everyone around you *appears* to be growing at a much faster rate. This brings me to a really important point. Please, please only concern yourself with what is happening for *you*. Treat all of your experiences with common sense, steering clear of any fantasy. And never, ever compete with another sitter in your group. That will inevitably cause resentment and jealousy, highly negative feelings that you cannot afford to invite into any circle.

'Is it all worth it?' I remember asking myself more than once, as I delved deeper and deeper into the world of spirit. Every student will ask themselves this question at least once at some point or other in their development, although how many times depends on the individual. Many leave their path the first time this question crops up, some even feeling sorry they started in the first place. As for me, I constantly had the feeling that I was somehow being held back. And I was. By *myself*.

Raising your Vibrations

In my early stages of development I would so often hear mediums, or even more advanced students than myself, say, 'You must learn to raise your vibrations.'

'Right,' I would think, 'raise my vibrations! Get the energy flowing! But how?'

When I would ask how to achieve this, I was never given a good answer. They all left me in the dark, literally. It was the first of many questions that remained unanswered for me. So I pass it along to you. Think about it. How can you raise your vibrations?

In any work with spirit, you must be prepared to meet spirit halfway. This means that you have to raise your own thought vibrations, gaining control of the mind. Therefore, it becomes very important to learn how to fill the mind with higher and better thoughts. By doing this, your auric vibration begins to accelerate, taking you away from the heavy, low levels of earthly mindsets such as fear, anger, worry and doubt.

By fully concentrating on positive, more compassionate thoughts – thoughts of healing others or of bringing good to people less fortunate than yourself – you will bring about a lightness of mind and a brightness of your own aura that will allow the spirit within you to become more apparent, thus allowing the spirit outside you to step closer and begin to forge the first real link with you.

Light Breaking Through

- For a moment, just try to imagine your spirit like a small, beautifully cut diamond shrouded in a mass of dark grey clouds. These heavy, overbearing clouds represent all of the doubts and fears that the mind has latched on to and collected for you over the years of your physical life.

- Now picture all around you, just outside the clouds, bright, beautiful sunlight. This crystal-clear brightness represents the beauty of the spirit world surrounding you, trying mightily to break through the cloud cover of the human mind.

- The first *true* spiritual experience you ever have will be when that spirit light makes contact with the diamond, filling you completely with light and colour. Then you will *know*. It works like a prism, sending out rainbow light all around it, melting away the darker memories and creating openings in your consciousness, letting in more of the higher spiritual nature.

I look at my own early journey through the various states of mind and realize that the mind can be just like the sea. Often it appears calm and inviting on the surface, but the real challenge is to find out what lies beneath the deep blue expanse. It is only when you can begin to bring calmness and a true clarity to the surface that you can begin to actually see beyond it and into the sea that is your consciousness. As long as you fear what lies at the depths, you will never progress to the next level of spiritual awareness.

OPENING UP

*'The best and most beautiful things in the
world cannot be seen or even touched –
they must be felt with the heart.'*
HELEN KELLER

This stage is about learning how to receive and understand
messages from the spirit world. You'll sometimes get feelings
and impressions that seem downright bizarre. That's fine –
it's a fun journey, after all, and sometimes a strange one
too! But it's also very rewarding, especially when you see
your efforts starting to pay off. However, there will be
many times, especially at first, when you will be unsure
of the messages and what spirit has to show you. Are they
real? Is spirit really giving this date or this name?

This part is about starting to work with spirit, being
guided by spiritual teachers and letting go and trusting in
the process...

4
Switching On and Off

'A flower seldom opens in the dark.'
DRONMA

The spirit world will not necessarily try to communicate with you each time you sit and close your eyes. But you can show that you are ready to receive messages by 'opening up' your mind and then 'closing down' when you have finished. Learning how to do this is a very important feature of mediumship development. I call it 'the art of switching on and off'.

There is no right way to switch on and off. In fact, there are probably as many methods as there are mediums. People will describe for you the different approaches they use, but it is up to you to choose the way that works best, and most naturally, for you. No matter which method you choose, it is imperative that you learn to do it very early on and that it becomes a mainstay to your practice. Here are a few ideas.

Switching On

First, you will need to find your own internal switch. Mine is a ritual prayer that I say in my head, directed towards people I know to be suffering mentally or physically. Thoughts of a compassionate nature will raise your own spiritual vibration and guide your mind upward in the direction of the higher, more spiritual forces.

Some people prefer a visualization, seeing themselves journeying into a higher state or place; others put out a call for guidance, or flick their switch by breathing deeply. As I said, the choice is yours, but some sort of mental tool is needed to guide you away from the lower physical concerns that surround your earthly being and open your consciousness to the higher levels of spirit around you.

This type of switch, or 'on/off' button, if used each and every time you sit in circle, will begin to act like a radio signal that your mind sends out to the spirit guides who are close to you. They, in turn, will act like receivers. The longer you practise sending out your signal, the stronger your transmission will become, and it will be so much better for you if you can send out from the same place at the same time each week.

This is why you should keep your development to the group or circle where you practise. To practise away from that place will only interfere with the mental connections you are strengthening with the spirit world. Also, the strong two-way link you have been forging, which will have been boosted by the conditions of the group almost like a battery, will not be at your disposal. Any information you can gain by practising away from the group is likely to be very much distorted in your early development.

Take Time for Yourself

It is important that you do *not* send out your signal each and every time you meditate. While you are developing, you need time for yourself as well as for spirit, and it's important to keep them separate. For years I have heard stories from people sitting in development circles claiming that the spirit world is interfering in their lives or disturbing them at home when they are trying to sleep or to meditate, and it's because they haven't learnt to switch on or off properly.

Also, sitting once a week is more than enough for anyone who is just starting out. Don't be fooled by the thought that the more often you sit, the more quickly you'll learn, or that somehow it will make you a better medium. All that will happen is that your mind will become crammed with thoughts and you won't know what is genuinely from spirit and what isn't. If you feel you must sit on your own at home, make good use of this time by meditating for yourself, to bring clarity to your mind and/or relaxation to your body.

Let Go and Trust

In your circle work, try, if you can, to get into a routine where you simply take each experience as it comes. There really is no point in trying to predict the next step of your development before it has happened. Each experience must be seen, then processed, and only when it is fully understood should you endeavour to proceed further. This way you eliminate unnecessary confusion and doubt from your mind.

Each little step further that you take requires the one key thing the student medium must attain if they are to go all the way on this journey: *trust*. The practice of meditation is important in developing such trust because we must first learn to hold the mind in place. To be accurate, though, what we are doing in circle is not strictly meditation. If meditation is about holding a focus within the mind, then the development of mediumship is really more about letting go. By this I mean that we are letting go of a part of our own space, allowing spirit to take control of the emptiness we have created. This is why the early part of your development contains so much meditation, clearing your emotions and learning to understand yourself. We need to know ourselves before we can truly let go.

Switching Off

Once you have learned how to switch on and mastered letting go and trusting, you are also required to *switch off*. Closing down, or switching off, is an almost natural occurrence. The highest energy point of the session will taper off naturally, the energy in the group will begin to fade and you will become more aware of the room around you and the people in it.

Even so, you should give yourself an exercise to end your practice. Again, a short prayer or visualization will suffice. I normally thank the spirit people for linking with me. That simple acknowledgement is enough for me to know that the link has been cut. Even a course of deep breaths followed by saying 'thank you' will do. There is no need to become dramatic with either switching on or off. Linking with the spirit world should be very graceful and natural. The important thing is that you acknowledge that your session is over.

I have witnessed some students hanging on for far too long at the end of a session, making a great show of coming out of the meditative state. Others have claimed that spirit would not let them go or stayed with them for days on end. If they only knew the amount of energy that would require, they would think differently! Whenever I take a class for developing mediums I always point this out. It is an indication to me that the developing medium is in fact hanging on to spirit, not the other way around.

So, for your own sake, and for the sake of the others sitting in your group, switch on at the start and please, please remember to switch off at the close.

Grounding Yourself

When you've finished doing your spiritual work, you should also go off and ground yourself by living your own life. You can't live your whole life 'spiritualized' – it doesn't work. Most people I've known who've had problems in psychic development – who've believed they were being followed by spirits or haunted as a result of their development – just hadn't grounded themselves properly. That's all there was to it. The 'haunting' wasn't because 'bad spirits' were around them but because their own head was messed up and they didn't know how to unplug, how to switch off from the spiritual side and have a human life.

Hauntings and so-called 'possessions' only occur in the human mind. They are human conditions, nothing to do with the spirit world, and often used, possibly unconsciously, as a way of gaining attention. But so often we don't know our own mind and that's why something deemed to be 'paranormal' can frighten us. But 99.9 per cent of the time, it's just us. That's another reason why it's so important to get to know ourselves and deal with our fears at the outset of our development. And then to switch off and ground ourselves after any spiritual work. If you do that each time, you will be fine.

I was fortunate that all the time I was doing my development I had a barber's shop and there was nothing more grounding than going in and giving someone a crew cut the next day! Whatever you do, balance your life in some way during the course of your development. Some people are grounded by their families, some by their work – whatever it is, it's important not to lose touch with everyday physical reality. If you find you're constantly thinking about your spiritual development – get grounded.

Your Space is your Own

And remember, *your space is your own*. No one and nothing can enter that space unless *you* allow it. The spirit world and those who dwell in it are completely free of this material world and lend themselves and their higher knowledge to those of us who seek that knowledge. It would make no sense if they were to try and hold on to physical matter, which they left behind many years ago, and have indeed gone far beyond.

The only thing that can hold on to your mind is your own fear. This is why I constantly tell people to be truthful to themselves in development and if they are afraid in any way of the idea of spirit holding on to them they should talk to the leader of their circle and openly discuss such fears. Talking about it will bring it out in the open and then it can be rationalized and understood. I do find it sad that people associate possessions and hauntings with the spirit world, when I know that the nature of spirit is to help, guide and heal.

5
Meeting your Guide

'When the student is ready,
the teacher will appear.'
BUDDHIST PROVERB

D o you need a guide to link with spirit? To first link with spirit, no, as you may have already found out for yourself, but as you develop you will encounter presences that you will grow to recognize as clearly as a friend or member of your family. These are your spirit guides.

Spirit Guides

There are many spirit guides and higher beings who come into our lives to steer us. So what are they exactly? Is there a band of spirit helpers alongside each and every one of us? Do they work separately, or occasionally in groups? And why are most of the guides you hear of Native Americans, Chinese medical practitioners or nuns?!

These are just a few of the questions frequently asked about spirit guides. Some of the answers I've heard through the years have been confusing and, dare I say it, sometimes even laughable. I shall try to simplify these questions for you and to give some examples of my own experiences of linking with higher spirits in the hope that it will make your understanding of these entities much clearer.

Spirit guides are said to be with us from birth; they are a bit like guardian angels. *Everyone* has some form of spiritual protection. How you view this protection, and interact with it, depends upon you. For a medium, it seems to be relevant for the guardian spirit, or guide, to make themselves known, as they control the work that mediums do from the spirit side. Also, from the medium's point of view, a spirit guide is a point of contact, a figure to relate to and a good focal point to attune to.

Your spirit guide will also act as your principal teacher. The further you go on your journey, though, the less you will need to refer to the physical presence or even the name of a guide. The more understanding you gain of your link with the spirit world, the less you will have to rely on physical references.

I have one spirit guide, and yes, I know it's almost a cliché, but he seems to be Chinese. I call him Chi. One night, some three years or so into my development, he appeared to me in my circle. While I was in a semi-state of trance, my mind was quite separate from my body and I could see a small figure of a man walking towards me. As he got closer, I could tell immediately that he was oriental. He seemed to take my hands and to lead me to a place that resembled a plateau at the top of a mountain.

The experience goes on and on, but the purpose of describing it for you is that Chi introduced himself to me as my spiritual guide and described his job to me as being my guardian at all times, working from his vantage point in the spirit world. Also, he said he would be in control of allowing in any other spirit being who wished to work with me. And he would be my principal teacher. The reason he made his appearance at that particular time was because he said I was ready.

Where Are Guides From?

It is quite common for people to have a guide that comes from a spiritually rich culture or background – a nun, a Native American, a Buddhist monk or another oriental figure. Many people have asked me why this is. It could be that the guide is someone who has lived on the earth plane in that form. However, some guides are not people who have lived on the earth plane, either in that form or even at all. Rather, they are spirit shaping itself to a specific need that we have, or into something that we perceive as holy. They are an archetype of what we perceive a higher self to be.

Guides often reflect life lessons too. They are there to illustrate what we need to learn as much as to guide us and to give us an easily recognizable connection to spirit. So they can be seen as more sacred beings, in a state to aspire to. It is a good feeling – a comfort and inspiration – to recognize that you have someone higher than you who can guide you.

A guide may have no apparent associations with anything in your life, but they are there and in that form for a very good reason that is worth reflecting on. For instance, you may have a Buddhist guide, even if you do not consider yourself a Buddhist. But you may nonetheless feel a connection with Buddhism, with the stillness and serenity that a Buddha has, and so be able to feel much more at peace when connected to your guide. Or not.

Here's an example that I witnessed for myself. There was quite a large gruff gentleman in circle who was trying to find his guide but was having quite a lot of trouble.

'A woman keeps appearing to me, but I'm not sure about her,' he said to his teacher. 'She's dressed like one of those Catholic nuns.'

'It could be your guide,' the teacher told him. 'It could be a nun.'

'But it can't be!' he exclaimed. 'I'm not Catholic!' He was negative about the Catholic Church because of his upbringing and it took him two years to accept his guide. In this way, your guide may reflect lessons you need in your life.

An Introduction to your Guide

If you would like to learn more about your own spirit guide, here's a meditation that I first gave on my CD *Developing Mediumship*:

Meeting your Spirit Guide

- First find yourself a relaxed position.

- Sit comfortably, feel relaxed and allow your body to become slow and still.

- Close your eyes.

- Start to pay attention only to your breathing. Breathe deeply in through your nose and pull the air deep into your body, all the while thinking of relaxing.

- Start to become aware of how the breath vibrates through your body, deep into the lungs.

- Follow the pulsing sensation, moving your lungs in and out, pushing energy all around your body.

- Concentrate solely on the rhythm of your body.

- Become aware of how heavy your body is becoming.

- As the body becomes heavier and you become more aware of it, equally watch the vibration in and around your body pulsing at a steady rate and in harmony with your blood flow.

- Start to look at the air coming into your body and concentrate on it being white, like a cloud of pure white energy sitting just in front of your face.

- Breathe it deep into your body and see it being pushed around your body, cleansing and cleaning, while all the while relaxing.

- Pull the white light into the darkest parts of your mind, deep within, filling them with light and energy, and all the while registering the pulsing of harmony moving through your body.

- Concentrate on how light this rhythm that's moving through your body is causing your mind to be.

- Sitting in the stillness of your own mind, surrounded by light, feeling the quietness of your own mind, you are becoming more comfortable in this state.

- This is the time when you can ask your spirit guides and teachers on the higher side to step closer to you, welcoming them into your space, your protected space of white light and silence.

- Try to become aware of any changes that are taking place around your body or in your body.

- Recognize any signs that the energies have changed.

- Start to become used to the sense of someone from the higher side entering into your space.

- Maybe you feel the vibration around your body quickening or feel the sensations of heat and cold around your body.

- Accept that this is the higher teachers changing the frequency around you.

- Try to become familiar with these changes. Each change is like a calling card from each different spiritual teacher who works with you.

- Feel the impressions that they are putting into your mind, impressions of who they are, when they lived, what they look like and what their intentions are in guiding you through your work.

- Try not to over-question in your mind, but accept the impressions that are given to you.

- Don't be in any rush to work out any understanding or meaning at this point. Just be in harmony with the guide and the stillness and light.

- Feel your mind lifting higher and becoming brighter as you link more completely with your spirit guide.

- Allow them to take you higher, more towards their frequency, and into a more spiritual state of being.

- Accept all the things that are shown to you at this point as coming from your spirit guide and from a much higher source.

- And start to feel yourself gently separating from the vibration of the higher spiritual guide, not clinging or holding, just releasing and allowing yourself to move back down through the light, pulling the light back towards your body, back to the centre of your being.

- And when you feel yourself filled with that light in your physical being, send out a note of thanks to that spiritual teacher who has allowed you to sit in their presence and has given you impressions and teachings of their life for your life's path.

- Breathing nice and deeply now, pulling air deep into your lungs and becoming more focused on the here and now, recognize that your physical body is sitting comfortable and relaxed.

- Become more and more focused and aware of the here and now. Recognize that your body is sitting still and that your consciousness is more in this waking state of physical reality.

- And when you feel ready, just take a nice deep breath and open your eyes.

Verification

It may be difficult to verify the existence of some of these spirit guides, so it is wise to look for some sort of confirmation. In fact, at the time of my own guide's appearance, I asked him to please confirm this to me. I had been asking for signs from my guide for some years before he deemed me ready to receive his presence.

The following evening I went along to one of the Glasgow churches to watch a demonstration of clairvoyance given by the great medium Albert Best. Albert, as usual, was in fine form, giving brilliant evidence of survival to many different people in the packed congregation. Suddenly he stopped for a moment and said, 'There is a young man at the very back of the church.' Pointing to me, he carried on, 'I have a message for you from someone in the spirit world.' Then he paused. 'Wait a minute, I never tell anyone about their own guides!'

Albert protested for a moment and then gave in and passed on the message. It was one of the briefest messages ever from the spirit world, but it was my first piece of confirmation from Chi. Just at the end of the short message Albert mentioned that the spirit guide would allow himself to be drawn for me. At the time I couldn't quite see how this could happen, so quickly dismissed it.

Five days later, I was introduced to a lady called Dronma. She was Buddhist and her name had been given to her by her Tibetan teacher. A short time after I had met this extraordinary lady, she told me that she could see my face changing, that I was beginning to look like an old Chinese man. I said nothing to her about my spirit guide and allowed her to give me a vivid description. In the middle of that description, she asked me if she could draw what she had just witnessed. Of course I agreed.

Would you believe it? A drawing was produced of the *very* Chinese guide whom I had met so recently and who had been described so accurately by Albert. I must add that before I had met Dronma, I hadn't known that she was an artist, or indeed that she was psychic. In fact, I had met her through one of my older brothers who had absolutely no interest in mediumship whatsoever.

This may not seem like concrete evidence, but for someone like Chi who lived such a long time ago and whose life is not documented in any way, this was the strongest corroborating evidence I could gain.

Over time I have learned of the existence of other guides and spirit teachers that Chi introduced me to and have verified them through their inclusion in history and reference books. It is important, where possible, to check up on any evidence given by those purporting to be your spirit guides or helpers. That will give you added confidence in them and in the process of receiving information from spirit.

Calling Cards

Just before Chi made himself known to me, I was becoming very confused. I was asking so many questions but not waiting for the answers, because my natural clairvoyant abilities were working without any proper guidance or instruction. I had been experiencing all kinds of psychic visions, so had been seeing all types of archetypal figures and asking each one if they were my guide. I felt ready to meet a guide and press on. A part of me felt as though I could rush through this development thing.

Chi, however, reminded me of something I had missed throughout my three years of sitting in circle: *he had been with me from the very outset.* How could I have missed this? How had I not received his *calling card*, if you like? Then I remembered the feelings I would get and dismiss – the sensations of having a fine wispy beard, wearing a robe and performing the type of *tai chi.* All the time my spirit guide had been trying to introduce himself to me, but I had been intent on looking elsewhere. Sometimes we just don't seem to see the wood for the trees, do we?

So please do try to take note of any sensation that occurs around your physical body whilst sitting with spirit. At first it may seem trivial or coincidental, but if the same sensation occurs time and time again, then it will be the sign of a spirit being projected onto your physical being for recognition – a spirit leaving their calling card.

Complete Spiritual Awareness

My mistake was to set limits on my sensitivity: I believed that I should *see* the spirit world, never thinking for a moment that I would be able to *feel* it. One of the main goals for any would-be medium is to expand into a *complete* spiritual awareness.

Those in spirit have since taught me that they will use my entire range of senses, if I am open to it. So now I am able to experience an almost complete sensation of the spirit person who is trying to communicate or link with me. So remember that the actual calling card of your spirit guide will eventually become known to you through all your senses.

In the beginning, you may feel the energy of the spirit to be quite intense. As you progress, your own vibration will adjust, allowing the link between you and the guide to become more and more gentle. It's not so different from breaking in a new pair of leather shoes, really. At first the intensity of the spirit may be uncomfortable, or feel somewhat tight, but in time their presence will become so comfortable that we will forget we are wearing them!

So now, before I do *any* kind of work as a medium, I wait to feel those sensations of Chi or the others that I recognize coming close to me, giving me the go-ahead to begin or a signal to stop. Whatever the instructions are, I do my best to follow them, for I know that they will never let me down. As long as I feel their calling card I know they are with me and that it is therefore safe to go ahead. If there is no sensation that I recognize, then I do not work: it's as simple as that. Mediumship requires a two-way connection and I wouldn't even want to attempt to give a sitting without the presence of my guide. Without a spirit presence it would be no more than a psychic reading.

Working with your Guide

Your guide will appear quite frequently when you first start, but as you develop more of your own connection with spirit, they will fade into the background. I am still in contact with Chi, but these days he rarely makes an appearance unless I am conducting a reading. Outside readings and sessions, he tends to appear when I have something new to learn, and more often when I am not paying attention to my current lessons in life and from spirit.

Remember that your guide is there to help you, not to do everything for you. At heart, you are forming your own connection with spirit, and your guides are there to help you build and sustain it, however they can. Ultimately, they are trying to bring you to the spirit *in you* – that's the only teaching that they're really there to give.

Unfortunately, people can become almost neurotically attached to spirit guides. That's not healthy. We should never depend on any other being like that. Guides are there to steer and help us along, that's all. I always instruct people not to cling to them.

Sadly, development circles are filled with claims of fanciful guides with colourful personalities, majestic clothes or special headgear. Some of them aren't even in human form. There was one woman I knew who believed her guide to be a walrus, and before she started any spiritual work she would kind of fluff up and then fall on the floor and roam around. And another had a *kipper* as a guide! Before she gave messages to people she would go very quiet and her mouth would open and close like a fish until she felt that the kipper guide was ready to work with her and then she would deliver messages in her own voice.

I would suggest that you do not get caught up in this type of behaviour. It's really not healthy! Treat your link with the spirit quite simply, and with respect. Don't make a game of it. Learn to know the signs of your particular guide and honour them.

Also, remember that those in spirit are actually pure energy, not people in body, even if they appear to you as such from time to time. They will come to you in whatever form your mind will accept. So if you are seeing some rather strange ones, maybe that's telling you something about your own mind. Everything comes back to yourself on your spiritual journey.

Keep It Simple

Simplicity is the order of the day when we reach this point on the journey; otherwise it will all become far too confusing. People can easily get carried away. Some start *becoming* their guides. They even start dressing like them. I had a very disturbing conversation once with a medium who said to me, 'My wife was really shocked when I told her that my Native American spirit guide was going to take over the driving of the car.' I was really shocked too!

When that sort of thing happens to you, go and clean the windows, hoover the carpet, dig the garden, *ground yourself.* And for goodness sake, don't let a spirit guide get behind the wheel.

Something else that people sometimes do is invent guides or helpers just to feel part of the crowd. If you attempt to do this, you are only deluding yourself. I waited three years in my circle before my guide properly introduced himself to me, but it was certainly worth the wait.

I have had discussions with people in the early stages of development who state that they have more than one guide – sometimes many more. Some people collect them – they're not content with one, they have a team. Then a tribe... But that's just complicating your mind. Remember, the idea on a spiritual journey is to make things *simpler.*

Over the course of your mediumship you may encounter different guides as you grow and need to learn new life lessons. You will also be shown different presences and personalities with the help of your guide. However, to have a lot of guides at once will often only be confusing; because of this, it is much more likely you will only have one. It is very important to know the difference between who your guide is and who is just coming through to give a message.

If you feel a whole tribe of guides is appearing to you at any point in the beginning of your development, I would advise that you link with spirit as a whole, rather than searching for a guide, and wait to let spirit show you who is your guide. Go back to the beginning. Retrace your steps. One presence will come through more strongly than any other.

Another point to be aware of is why you need to have all of these guides. Are they aspects of your own mind? It can tell you a lot about your own thinking.

So, remember, don't invent them, don't have too many and don't let them drive.

Many Guides, Many Lessons

Having said this, at times I have met more than one spiritual guide. Each of them was there to impart a particular lesson and they faded once I had grasped what they wished to teach me. This may happen to you too. If you needed to become more devoted to your work, for example, you could be helped by someone who had lived their life with complete devotion to a cause: a nun or monk, perhaps.

Each new helper who was brought forward to meet me had a different calling card from my original guide, but it was always Chi's sensation I would be aware of at first. Just as he had promised on our first meeting, he would always be the main guide for me.

As I began to recognize the different spirits who came to work with me, I also recognized changes in myself.

For example, Chi seemed to appear when I most needed balance in my life. Then he would introduce me to a spirit helper of a different nature, who in turn would inspire me to learn new things from their own particular discipline. For example, Chi's teaching to me was always about how to become more disciplined and calm in my life. The next helper he brought along taught me devotion, which was a reflection of that particular individual's life here on earth.

As I embraced the changes in myself, my mediumship also changed, moving onto a much deeper level. I was finally learning to let go, and the more I could let go and trust, the clearer things became. Each new spirit teacher Chi brought to me would pass on a teaching of their own – either about themselves, or about mediumship, or in many cases about me and how I could grow further as a person – and all the while my link with the spirit world was becoming stronger. As I became more aware of the spirits, I was learning to trust them and the messages they brought for me.

Let the Link Grow ... Gently

This is a very exciting stage of spiritual development, when you feel like a spiritual child whose eyes have just been opened up for the first time. Suddenly you witness the splendour of a beautiful new land that lies before you, filled with majestic sights just waiting to be discovered. When you reach this point, it will remind you of the very beginning and how excited you felt. Except that now your awareness will have been opened up and your material thoughts will have lessened as you have built up knowledge and understanding of the world of the spirit that you are so much a part of. As your mind gains clarity, you will become aware that there is much more you want to know and do.

Above all, your contact with spirit will fuel you. It immediately gives a complete feeling of wellbeing and security. It is because I have connected with this that it has become extremely important for me to take and communicate that energy to others. The enthusiasm and desire to bring that same kind of upliftment to others in itself is such a positive feeling. While the messages are important, I believe any medium should ultimately be looking for that connection so that they can not only understand whom and what they are working with, but also be able to communicate that effectively through the messages they receive.

Once again I caution you to be patient at this time. When you are required to work for spirit and to share your gifts with the world, you will be the first person to find out. Even with the best will in the world, do not run around trying to heal people, giving them messages from their relatives in the spirit world or spouting great diatribes of some new-found spiritual philosophy. If you do, you'll appear something of an extremist and other people will not understand your enthusiasm; in fact, some may think you mad.

The world is not ready for wannabe mediums practising unrefined psychic or spiritual abilities at whim, all in the name of spirit. Allow the link you have found to grow and wait for your next instruction. You will learn with time that mediumship requires great patience, not 'gushy' enthusiasm. You are an instrument that information passes through, that's all. So relax, be patient and trust that you will be told when the time is right to begin your practice in the world.

6
Trust

'Our truest life is when we are in dreams awake.'
HENRY DAVID THOREAU

Trust, which I cannot emphasize too strongly in this book, is in fact your next valuable lesson. Once you begin to establish a link with the higher levels of spirit, you must work to build a bridge of trust with one another. Question the spirits as much as you feel you have to; ask for more guidance or clarity if need be. If you are truly linked, they will always try to let you know of their authenticity. Only when you are satisfied with the alliance should you continue to the next level of mediumship.

The Language of Spirit

By this time in your development, the link you can form should be making you more aware of the true sensations of the spirit. This is a much more intuitive level of understanding, which engages our ability to sense emotion at a level that takes us deeper inside ourselves. It is here that we must learn to trust the most, remembering that the language of spirit is in thoughts and feelings – a telepathic language which by now you should be beginning to understand almost organically.

We read the language of spirit through our feelings and sensations, not through our five physical senses. This may take some time to perfect. Up to this point, most of the communications will have been played out in your imagination, sort of like daydreams you have had to interpret. Working at this new level of feelings and sensations not only brings a new vibrancy and intensity, but a whole new reality. Now the spirit world becomes *real*. Are you ready for this?

If you have travelled this far on your path, then it is likely that you will be prepared to move into this reality with ease. However, any form of true mediumship demands that the medium shows great trust in letting go of their own space and allowing a higher being to occupy it. The extent to which you can vacate your space determines how much room you will give over to spirit control.

One thing I have always said is that everyone can find a link to spirit, but there are many different ways and many different links. It is like entering an art class. Some people will be natural painters, while some will find their niche in sculpture or drawing. Similarly, there are different ways of working as a medium.

Types of Mediumship

Most people assume that mediums are there simply to give messages from people from the other side on a public platform, but mediumship covers a much wider area. As I've already mentioned, not everyone who studies mediumship will end up on a platform; indeed, I was trained as a healer before I was sent by Mrs Primrose to work publicly.

As you develop, you will, over time, lean towards a specialization as you gain more experience of working with spirit and start to feel an affinity towards one or more areas.

Healing

First, and most significant, is healing. In this sense I mean the shifting of energies to take away pain or correct an imbalance in a person. However, *every* aspect of working with spirit involves healing of some sort.

Mental Mediumship

Second is mental mediumship. This is the mediumship most commonly associated with public platform work and private readings, and involves delivering spirit messages to people.

Trance Mediumship

Trance mediumship is where the medium's body is 'overshadowed' and then controlled by spirits in order to deliver messages.

Physical Mediumship

Closely related to trance mediumship is physical mediumship, where spirits control the medium's body and produce physical phenomena such as apports, objects that appear out of apparently nowhere, or transfiguration, where a spirit shapes the medium's appearance to an approximation of how they looked when they were alive. Also materialisation, where a substance called ectoplasm exudes from the entranced medium's body and can allow the spirits to take on their form or human appearance. Both these are very rare nowadays.

Teaching

Finally, you may grow to become an excellent tutor, teaching others both about the spirit world and about themselves. It is important to remember that any teaching you receive from spirit will be appropriate to you at your level: a university professor of physics will not try and teach schoolchildren!

With knowledge of these states, you can start to find where your talents lie, where you have been called by spirit to work for the benefit of all. If you wish to remain almost fully aware of the physical world, then overshadowing will suffice, as often happens with clairvoyance and clairaudience. If, however, you are more able to let go and trust, you will be guided into a safe state of trance.

So, how do we go deeper? How do we give spirit the best chance of working with us, to the fullest extent possible? The simple but elegant answer is to *trust more*. Make more room. Each person will do this in their own way.

If you have been able to stay the course thus far and worked through all of the growing pains of spiritual childhood, then now would be a good time to attempt to practise working out your own particular spiritual gifts. The very fact that you might have come this far says something special about you. As you sit in your development circle each week, you will now need to practise letting the spirits bring *their* gifts *through* you to those who are most in need of them.

7
Overshadowing

*'How can you have shadows
if you do not have light?'*
GORDON SMITH

I t is my belief that all mediums working for the higher
spirit are in some way overshadowed by spirit beings
during the process. It would seem that the closeness of the
spirit control to the medium determines the strength of the
mediumship. Overshadowing determines the strength of
communication coming through from the other side.

Letting Go and Switching On

Earlier in this book I talked about letting go, giving up a
certain amount of consciousness in order that the controlling
spirit working with you can gain more command of your
psyche and use more of your faculties. In all the forms of
mediumship I have demonstrated, I have consciously let go
of a part of myself, leaving space for the particular control

to occupy. This is the linking point, where the medium switches on.

Learning to allow yourself to be overshadowed by spirit at the outset of development is the foundation for all that you will do in future. Whether you develop all the way to deep trance work or remain at the mental levels of mediumship such as clairvoyance or even spiritual healing will depend upon how far you let go. It is the difference between strong specific mediumship and poor psychic intuition based on mind-reading and other associated guesswork.

Overshadowing is the one true element that distinguishes a medium from a psychic reader. For that reason alone it must be developed to the full if you wish to practise as a medium.

When we first learn to link with spirit and begin to realize that we are being overshadowed by controls or guides, we tend to think that's it. In fact, it is only the start. These feelings of linking should be understood as being the same set of feelings that we will experience each time we use our mediumship.

If in the future you ever feel that you have become lost in your work, then refer back to the moment when you first established a link with spirit – that first point of overshadowing. Not only will you find your direction, but you will also remind yourself that it is spirit doing the work, using you as the channel. Far too many mediums forget this crucial distinction.

The degree of overshadowing possible depends upon the conditions of the medium, the sitter and the place of demonstration. It can develop into full trance.

Trance

Trance is noticeably different from overshadowing. Perhaps the most important distinction is that it is much rarer these days, partly because of the level of effort needed. The practice requires a much greater level of devotion and commitment than mental mediumship.

For the new student coming into development for the first time, trance mediumship is a long way off. Please remember this and honour it. The discipline required for this advanced channelling method will take many, many years to develop and much specialized preparation, not to mention extraordinary patience. This is primarily because every member of the circle needs to overcome all their individual fears and doubts about it. And almost everyone has them when they first witness such an altered state. Believe me, when the energies start to change as someone shifts into trance, it can be frightening, and unlike anything you encounter in your everyday life. So you have to adapt to this, and it will take time.

'Taster' Trances

During the course of your development you may experience short episodes of trance states, especially if you have learned to let go enough to be overshadowed. But do remember such events during early learning are no more than a foreshadowing of the practice. Spirit will try it out on each sitter in a circle, testing them in order to gauge how far each student is willing to travel.

In my experience I was taken many times into deeper and deeper states of overshadowing before finally being allowed to go down into complete trance. Even then, the trance experiences were brief, to say the least! At first I only encountered quick glimpses of what I might be used for if I showed an ability to remain at ease in body and mind while in this state. By the time I began to develop my mediumship at this level, I had trained my mind for almost four years. Needless to say, I was still at an embryonic stage.

Many people starting out confuse overshadowing with deep trance. I seem to remember sitting for about five years in 'stage two', building my link with spirit in my circle before they even attempted to take me into this advanced state. You, too, may experience many different levels of trance or overshadowing randomly in your development. This does not mean to say that you have been earmarked for that type of work. Accept each thing as it comes and only when there is repetition beyond coincidence can you expect to be taken in this direction.

The first time I went through this experience, I naturally hoped and believed that it would happen to me each time thereafter. This just did not happen. If anything, the trance state didn't occur again for me for at least another six months, teaching me once again never to assume that just because spirit chooses to use you for something once it will necessarily become a part of how they want you to work with them in future.

As has now become quite clear, the development of trance can and does take many years to perfect. My own teacher sat for 15 years in circle before she was accepted to work in this way and thought nothing of it. In the meantime, she refined her abilities as a mental medium and as a spiritual healer. Fortunately for me, I only sat for seven-and-a-half years to reach the same level. This does not say so much about me, but more about my gifted teacher, who knew best how to nurture me along.

Overshadowing vs Trance

There is a notable difference worth defining here between letting go for trance and being open to overshadowing.

No matter how advanced the overshadowing might become, the medium will at all times be aware of their physical senses.

In trance, they may be required to let go completely of any control of the physical vehicle, allowing the consciousness to be suspended in an animated state. This is a bit like going into a voluntary coma. I say 'voluntary' because the medium will have been building up trust with spirit in circle for some years before this type of situation will ever arise and, like my own experiences, will have had many practices before the actual trance link is perfected.

A 'Quick Fix'

Proper trance mediumship, in my view, is very rare today. I believe this is due to several factors, but mainly because most people who venture into mediumship these days show no patience and lack the commitment required to attain such a high standard of work with spirit. Sad as it is to say, most people would rather have the quick development fix, hoping that it will propel them rapidly onto the public platform, than make a commitment for the long haul. After a short period of time, these people always come unstuck.

I am reminded of one of my favourite stories, which appeared in one of my previous books, *The Unbelievable Truth*. It happened back in the late 1960s in Glasgow to a woman I shall call Joan for the purposes of this story.

Joan went along to a Spiritualist church as she had become interested in the subject and felt that she was a bit psychic herself, and she was quite surprised to receive a message from the medium on her first visit. The medium told her that she was indeed psychic and should learn to develop her gift in a development class. After the service finished she gave her the name and address of a woman she should go to to develop her gift.

Joan arrived at the house the following Thursday evening. Standing outside the front door she felt a little apprehensive, but eventually she knocked on the door, which opened almost at once and there stood a very frail-looking elderly lady. Joan thought she must be the medium who would train her, but the little old lady told her that she was only there to make tea for all of the people who sat together in the group. She showed Joan into the front room of the house. About 10 people were sitting in a circular formation and there was one empty chair, which Joan was ushered towards by a very large, roundly built lady who called out, 'Ah, you must be Joan. Come and sit by me and when we are all ready we shall begin to meditate.'

Joan sat down and wondered, 'How do you meditate?' No one explained what to do and she was too scared to ask, so she just closed her eyes and thought about anything she could for the next half-hour.

Finally the large lady beside her called out in a loud voice, 'Stop meditating now and tell me what you witnessed during your meditation.'

Joan panicked, as she had only thought about things that she had to do at home, but as they went round the group and she listened to some of the rubbish being spoken, she decided to copy them and say she was off on a spiritual journey.

'Joan, tell me what happened to you now,' demanded the big lady.

'I saw an Indian gentleman dressed in lots of feathers,' Joan lied.

'An Indian in feathers! Well, I shall expect great things from you in the future,' the big lady said.

She then explained to the group that she was about to go into a very deep trance and that she required everyone to be completely silent as she could be injured or even killed if any member of the group moved or made a sound.

Joan sat holding her breath, watching as the big lady started to gyrate and wobble. With the weird sounds she was making, it seemed as though she was having a fit. Then, without warning, she jumped to her feet, hands outstretched, and started to talk in a very forced deep voice.

'Welcome, earthlings! I come from the planet Uranus and I come to give you advice about your planet.'

Joan's eyes almost popped out of their sockets. Then, at that very moment, this gem of trance philosophy was interrupted by the door opening slowly. For a moment Joan was afraid of what might be coming in, but it turned out to be the old tea lady, who paid no attention to the big lady in the trance and went around the circle of people asking what they would like on their sandwiches. Joan watched her slowly make her way around the group until she stopped behind the big medium and whispered, 'What would you like on your sandwiches, cheese or ham?'

As quick as a flash the big lady's head turned and she broke her trance for a second and shouted loudly, 'Ham!'

No more needs to be said, really. The truth is that this would never happen. A trance state simply cannot be interrupted and returned to – the level of relaxation needed is not something that can be snapped back and forth. Even after many years of work, mediums can find it tiring to channel so thoroughly.

Physical Mediumship

Physical mediumship is even more rarely encountered these days, unlike the early days of Spiritualism, when the materialization of spirits in séance rooms attracted the attention of many of the eminent minds of those times.

This type of mediumship can only be attained after a very long period of development and takes intense dedication. The effect on the medium's physical body is enormous and it takes an utterly selfless individual who is generous in heart and mind to allow their body, mind and spirit to be used in this way. The phenomenon itself has decreased in the last 40 years and nowadays there are not many groups sitting for physical phenomena and even fewer mediums willing to commit themselves to such lengthy training.

I myself have not sat for physical mediumship, although I have met and sat with mediums who have. Mrs Primrose, my original spiritual teacher, and the great medium Albert Best both told me of their times in early development circles. Both witnessed the materialization of spirits through the famous medium Helen Duncan and others, and both agreed that it was a phenomenon of its time, created by the power of emotion experienced during the Second World War, when people were dying *en masse*.

Even in those extreme times physical mediumship was considered very rare and required great dedication. Although neither Mrs Primrose nor Albert developed it themselves, both sat in circles where it did take place and they told me how disciplined you had to be to get in and of how these circles were strict and strenuous in ways that modern people could not imagine. In those days each sitter was expected to arrive each week at the same time and take their place with no thought of ever being late or absent. Such infractions were considered entirely unacceptable and could lose people their valuable place in these groups.

I would recommend that you put any thoughts you may have of becoming a physical medium to the back of your mind. I know from extensive experience that natural physical mediums are very rare indeed, and even in the past, when due to the phenomenon being more common, teachers were more abundant, considerable time was required for proper development.

In any case, I am pleased to say that mediumship today has moved on to a different level in terms of venue and acceptability, leaving behind darkened séance rooms for well-lit churches, town halls, theatres and even major city arenas. In effect, we have now bridged the gap from secrecy to sharing. It is through mental mediumship and healing that the majority of people now hear the message that you cannot die for the life of you. However, though ways of demonstrating spirit's existence have changed, commitment should still be the most important aspect of developing mediumship.

8
The Practice

*'With realization of one's own potential
and self-confidence in one's ability,
one can build a better world.'*
THE DALAI LAMA

Like any course you have taken in life, there is nothing
greater than putting into practice what you have
learned. And when you are ready, you are likely to add
a practice group to your work with your development
circle.

This is a bit like moving from the last year at primary
school to the first year at secondary. Even though you may
feel you have come a long way, and indeed you have in
several respects, somehow you find yourself at the beginning
again. This is just the way of spiritual development; growth
is constant, and at times there does not seem to be an end.
But being allowed to practise any form of mediumship
seems to bring its own rewards.

Healing

My leap from circle took me into a healing group. Even though I was still attending my circle on a Thursday night, I had been asked by Mrs Primrose to join a class for healing on a Tuesday night. It was during this time that I felt I was truly beginning to settle down. No more questions, no more asking for proof of the spirit world. Finally, I was actually going to be allowed to practise my spiritual gift of healing. What was even better was that I hadn't asked to do this myself. Instead the group leader, in all of her wisdom, had encouraged me, approaching me with the idea herself.

When I had started out on this path, I had wanted very much to be a medium, standing up on the platform giving people messages from their loved ones in the spirit world. I had never even considered that I might perform healing. And yet, my time in the healing group was one of the best periods of my development. I couldn't wait for Tuesday evenings to arrive. In all of my time with that group, five years, I think I only missed one session.

I also think I learned more from practising healing than from any other part of my development as a medium. I was still the needy child seeking attention until I started healing. Then I really started focusing on other people and developing compassion. This particular period in my development is the one I look back on most fondly, and it is the time when I felt most contented. I'm sure anyone who does healing work will tell you the same. It is one of the most precious gifts of the spirit that there is. To see the upliftment that you can bring to a person who is suffering is a wonderful thing.

As a probationary healer, I had to work with one of the most experienced members of the group, whose job it was to teach me the dos and don'ts of the gift. I know that I put my heart and soul into it and welcomed every opportunity to give.

Like most gifts of the spirit, healing is natural to those who channel it, so the best thing a teacher can do is allow the pupil the freedom to express their own abilities in this field, in effect acting as something of an overseer. Thankfully, that's what my healing teacher did for me, and within a short period of time I was working on my own. My eagerness was such that I wanted to cure instantly everyone who was brought to me.

Absent Healing

The first lesson I learned in healing was in absent healing – not being with a person needing healing but focusing thoughts and prayers on them. I was fortunate enough to achieve some great results that way.

One night I was doing some absent healing on my own father, who suffered a lot in his life from arthritis and asbestosis. I was visualizing myself in his room, and I was doing it so strongly that I could hear his voice and see my own hands like light going over his body. And then suddenly I shot back to my own room and thought, 'What happened?' And my father rang me and said, 'I just had this dream that you were standing beside me, waving your hands over me!' He also told me that after waking from the dream he went back to the deepest and most peaceful sleep he'd had in years.

If you would like to try some absent healing, here's a meditation, from my CD *The Healing Power of Mediumship*, that you can use to channel healing energy to others, either close by or at a distance.

Practising Absent Healing

- First of all, relax, sitting comfortably with a straight back.

- Close your eyes.

- Start to breathe, nice and deeply, in through your nose, filling your stomach with air and letting go of any tensions, any anxieties, that may be in or around the body.

- Be aware of your breathing and allow it to become steady and sure.

- Follow the air in through your nose, down into your solar plexus, to the centre of your being.

- And here, visualize a clear-cut diamond, rotating in a clockwise fashion.

- Follow the breath down to that diamond and allow it to rotate, steadily, in a clockwise fashion.

- Be aware that your body is relaxing as you sit, and become aware of how grounded your body has become.

- Send out a thought to the higher spirits around you, asking them to step into your space.

- Start to become aware of a finer vibration around your own body.

- Feel the vibration of your own spirit being as it merges with those from the higher side.

- And ask if they will lend you that clear pure spirit light to send out to any whom you know to be suffering in this world.

- Opening up your crown centre, accept that you can be used as a channel for healing and ask them to pour down a pure clear spirit light into the very heart of your being, where the diamond is turning slowly in a clockwise fashion.

- Feel yourself being filled by this pure clear spirit light.

- And visualize one whom you know to be sick or suffering at this time.

- Try to fix their image in your mind, to see their illness or their fear, to see that which holds them back in this life.

- And send out a beacon of light from the diamond at the centre of your being.

- Send out that light in their direction and surround them with the healing power of spirit.

- See them being bathed in that light and allow it to go to the heart of their problem.

- Hold this focus for as long as you feel necessary.

- And start to recall the light back towards your own centre, feeling this clear spiritual energy heading back towards you, moving back towards the diamond at your centre, moving back through the diamond and upwards, up out of your crown, back into the universe.

- Close down your crown centre.

- Feel the diamond dissolve into your very being, knowing that the healing that you have given out has also affected you.

- Be at one with yourself.

- Know that what you have asked for has been done.

- And start to focus on your breathing. Breathe nice and gently, pulling air back into your body and becoming more focused on the here and now.

- And with each in-breath you become more awake.

- And recognize where you are sitting.

- And recognize the room that you started in.

- And when you're ready, open your eyes.

You will gain much satisfaction from healing. It tells you that things can be made well. Where there is doubt and darkness, you can bring light and hope. You can become almost like an emotional lifeguard, pulling people out from their riptides and undercurrents.

Protect Yourself

Do safeguard yourself when you act as an emotional lifeguard, though – don't jump in or you can get swept away as well. It is possible to sympathize so much with a person's suffering that you can take on the symptoms of their condition and carry them way beyond the healing. I've been to the doctor's myself with acute angina and arthritis of the knee, neither of which I had. But I had been healing a woman with angina and healing my father's arthritic knee. If you're not careful you can end up being a sponge that sucks up people's hurts and pains – and sometimes it doesn't even help the patient, such can be the need of the healer to take the suffering onto themselves. So remember the pain is not yours: you are there to balance and brighten the energies of the patient.

Here again you have to take care to open up, do your work and then close down. Some people have cleansing rituals that they use after healing. Work out what's best for you. What I do is ask spirit to come and help and then afterwards say thank you. I used to make it more dramatic, but I've stopped that now. That was more about me than about spirit!

Developing Psychic Awareness through Healing

It's often through healing someone, or even just the desire to heal them, that we develop a spiritual link with them and are able to tune in to what's going on in their lives. I used to go so deep while healing that I was beginning to tune in to the spirit people around the patient. Instructed by my leader never to give clairvoyant messages to patients, or to diagnose illnesses, I was never able to find out if the impressions I was picking up were right or wrong. Despite my eagerness, I now see that my teacher was quite correct. Even if what I was getting was accurate, I was still too inexperienced to deliver such messages to the public. After all, it was still only four years since I had begun my development.

But it's amazing what you're able to pick up from someone without any words. Often it's not just the illness that's bothering them but a loss they've had some time ago. It was through picking up on such things that I was able to build compassion for people. Healing was a very good discipline for me.

I've found in teaching other people that the best way to develop your psychic awareness is to have a goal: the goal of helping people. Otherwise the process can be so random, with predictions and all kinds of psychic phenomena happening all over the place. That's why it's good to have some structure, some knowledge of how to access and direct your link to spirit – and above all that intention behind it.

And remember, whatever good is done for the spirit world is done and then forgotten. That way it lasts forever. If you keep it for yourself, it's no good. The more we learn to let go, the more comes through us.

Dedication

As with all areas of development, whether in a circle, a group for clairvoyance and psychic practices or a healing session, how dedicated you are can determine how adept you will become. Dedication and devotion are among the most important features of your spiritual work.

One of the old healers, John Keenan, would often take me aside and impart little nuggets of wisdom gleaned from his vast experience and many years of helping people. One thing I remember he used to say to me was, 'What you put in is what you will get out.' I do believe he was right.

I do consider myself very fortunate to have been guided by such dedicated people as John, Albert, Mrs Primrose and many others who put so much into their work for spirit.

The Pioneers

Within the modern movement of Spiritualism, people talk of how good the mediums and healers of the olden days were compared to those of today. Back then, the world moved at a slower pace and people had fewer distractions in their lives. Mediums and healers really did dedicate themselves to their work. They toiled tirelessly to bring Spiritualism to where it is today. Now, mediums are fortunate to be able to work in proper churches and centres as a result of the valuable groundwork those early pioneers laid down. I myself practised my early healing in one such place – the little local Spiritualist church.

Taught themselves by dedicated people of that bygone generation, our teachers instilled in all of us their knowledge and all of the wisdom they had gained from the days when mediums like Helen Duncan were performing séances in private houses to allow the spirits to fully materialize for their loved ones and when great healers were curing all kinds of illnesses in the name of the spirit.

If during your journey, you haven't already studied some of the past exponents of Spiritualism, now would be a good time to do it. Those who have gone before you may inspire you, or at least give you some understanding of the standards you should be aiming for with your own spiritual work. Do *not*, whatever you do, try to emulate them. They had their gifts and you have yours. Instead, just read their stories and try to appreciate what they went through and how much they ultimately achieved. Spiritualist libraries are filled with books on great pioneers like Ena Twigg, D. D. Home, Arthur Findlay, Helen Duncan and Albert Best.

Pause and Reflect

On this special journey it is very difficult not to become extremely excited about the work, or the development, or all of the wonderful teachings that you learn. But, like that child who has been promoted from primary to secondary school, there comes a moment when it is time to grow up. And as you begin to practise any of the spiritual gifts, you must develop tact, discretion, humility and dignity, as well as become accustomed to using good common sense and maintaining a sense of decency. All of this is crucial before you ever begin to share your gifts with the public.

If this is where you find yourself on your spiritual path, now would be a good time to pause and reflect on the past few years.

A Self-Awareness Moment

Having been on your spiritual journey for a while now, take a look back and consider how you have grown as a person.

- Are you less afraid of this life than when you took your first step in development?

- Do you react more calmly in stressful situations now?

- Do you consider other people's feelings more than you used to?

- Do you worry less about the future and care more for the here and now?

- Are you more content with your life and what you have than when you first began?

- Do you feel more in touch with your own emotions?

- Do you know how to bring balance to your mind when there is uncertainty?

- Do you think less of dying and care more for living?

- And do you feel lighter of mind now?

If the answer to these questions is a resounding 'Yes!', then you are beginning to transform yourself. Your mind is relaxing and peace is something you can realize instead of pray for. Your consciousness is expanding in the correct way, and even though life will still have some hurdles ahead of you, you are prepared for whatever is in front of you.

STAGE THREE
DELIVERY

'And the day came when the risk to remain tight in a bud was more painful than the risk it took to blossom.'

ANAÏS NIN

So, if you have followed your intuition and attended an appropriate circle or group…

If you have embarked on a course of spiritual development involving opening up your latent gifts of mediumship…

If you have examined your own mind and the emotional entanglements of this life…

If you have cleared out the dark rooms of your mind and become psychologically robust...

And learned to trust in your new-found ability to form a link with spirit...

Then you not only deserve some sort of medal, but deserve to call yourself a medium-in-the-making, at the very least!

This stage is about learning when you are ready to deliver and learning how to deliver spirit messages in a loving, fulfilling way, both in public and in private readings.

9
Reality Check

*'Our greatest fear is not that we are
insignificant – our greatest fear is that
we are powerful beyond measure.'*
MARIANNE WILLIAMSON

Before you move on, take the time to take a breather
and reflect on what you have achieved and where
you are now. You have already – I hope – realized that
you have grown into a stronger, more emotionally and
psychologically robust person, better able to deal with the
challenges ahead. Try now to ready yourself for the work
that is to come.

Take heart from all that you have learned. This includes
not only making a bond with the higher spiritual forces, but
through your meditation and practices of self-awareness,
you have also become more attuned to the world around
you and the world of spirit. Your own understanding of the
human psyche should have grown considerably and most
of the fears and anxieties with which you started out on

this journey will have been conquered. Above all, you will have learned about love and compassion – for others, and for yourself.

Service to the Public

You will probably understand by now that this journey is a difficult one, because – not unlike the military! – you are totally and utterly focused on making preparations for what is to come, yet you do not really have any idea what may be on the horizon. Strangely enough, you really may not be so very different from the young cadet in the army who has committed his life to helping others and knows in his heart that he wants to serve, but often feels he has taken on far too much in the way of rigorous training. Only once he finds himself in the uncertainties of the theatre of war does he realize, and *wish*, he could have learned so much more.

Being a medium can be a thankless task at times. Yet being allowed to be the giver of hope to the hopeless and healing to the heart that is breaking is a rare privilege indeed. I feel extremely fortunate in having the opportunity to bring a glimmer of light into the lives of people who are suffering, and I have never taken this gift for granted, or treated it lightly, or in jest.

However, that is not to say that a medium cannot have a sense of humour! In fact, I am often told that one of the reasons people perhaps warm to my messages is that I don't treat it all too seriously. I respect it, absolutely, but I never feel compelled to remain stern and unsmiling, as though delivering a university lecture in pursuit of tenure. If those in spirit communicating messages are cheeky or irreverent by nature, then that is what I will bring through. I do not edit out anything that seems a bit silly or off the wall.

Believe me, those in spirit know *what* they want to say and they know *how* it will resonate with the intended recipients. It is not up to me to make that call. Besides, it is often said that laughter is the best medicine, and there are times when those in the spirit world know that that is exactly what is needed, not only for the listener, but perhaps for the whole congregation, and even for me!

The knowledge you gain from platform work is as rich and important to your development as any work in circle, because each message is new. If you allow spirit to work, they will teach you something new on every single level, every single time.

This applies equally with a private sitting, though the energy is different here than when working in public. Working in private has a much more sombre tone; as a medium, you are working with one person's need, and it is intense. There is rarely a 'high' energy to work from, though there is a high expectation. It's a much more focused working and, unlike public workings, where you have a wide possibility of people to give a message to, you have nowhere to turn if you get any details wrong. You just have to go back in your mind to your guide and ask for more clarity.

Even though you may at this time be preparing to work for the spirit world, you should definitely remain in your circle. Development does not end because you have begun to practise the skills. Leaving your foundation circle now would be like leaving school at the age of ten. Consider, if you will, that the spiritual work you are going to do in the near future is like a day release from college: it is a practical exercise to further your knowledge while improving your skills. Never try to run before you can walk!

10
Giving Private Readings

*'And ever has it been known that love knows not
its own depth until the hour of separation.'*
KAHLIL GIBRAN

Your first attempts at practising mediumship, in
whatever form, will usually come as a great relief to
you. All of the spirit energy that has been building up
within you throughout your early training will at last be
allowed to be vented.

But have patience. Don't be in any kind of hurry. Just
wait openly and patiently for the instruction from spirit.

Where a medium starts is entirely down to the way
the development circle is run and where they are being
instructed to go by spirit. This is another reason why trust
is so, so important.

You will know you are ready to give private readings
from the level and quality of content you are giving in
circle. You are also likely to have been told by spirit that
you are ready to do this.

Giving private readings is a great discipline. It is one of the best learning tools available. You are in a situation where someone has had a loss and you have to tune into that person. So a private sitting is much more intense than a circle.

Communication

Whether your first practice is giving a private reading or going on a public platform, communication is one of the biggest parts of mediumship – drawing people to you and communicating in such a way that they are willing to unload their sufferings. People are usually frightened to do that, especially to a stranger, so you must be able to give them confidence.

Part of communicating in this way is to listen not to the words that people are saying as much as to the sounds that they are making. In this way you can tap into the feelings behind the words and gain more awareness about how the people are feeling. Forget the words, listen to the sounds. The language of the developing medium is a language of empathy, of compassion, of feeling.

You also have to look at the people who are coming to you. Sceptics will say that mediums look at people and tune in to their body language. There are times when that's true, because you are using your sight for that very reason – to tune in to that person. When you are learning to do readings, really study the person you're going to do a reading for. Really look at them. As humans we're used to wearing masks, but actually we can see through people's masks if we take the time to look – and especially if we take the time to look with compassion and the intention to help. Then there's a good chance of seeing behind the mask and guiding them out of whatever suffering they are in.

In observing people over the years I've learned to recognize someone who's had a loss. That's nothing psychic, it's just learned behaviour. They even carry themselves differently with different types of loss – murder, for example, or a long drawn-out illness. You can see that from their demeanour, without even asking spirit. With murder there's usually an icy anger, which they may not even recognize; with a long-drawn-out illness, a type of exhausted grief where they have given so much of their own energy to the person that was dying that they now need to recover and reconnect to the person they've lost on a different basis. Over time you learn to pick up on these things. It becomes easy to tell whether a person's lost a child, partner, parent or friend just from seeing them walk into the room for their reading.

Your Intention

The first thing that needs to be focused on is your intention to help that person. Don't forget that. You're not there for yourself, you're there for the people who have come to you. You're there to help them. Mediumship is a tool to heal the hearts of the bereaved. Your intention should always be to lift people out of their grief – not to be seen as a clever person who has some kind of gift.

So ask mentally, 'May I serve today?' or 'Can I be allowed to help this person today?' Focus on your feelings and look out for a sign.

If you suddenly feel a presence around you, for example, or a feeling of joy, continue as you would in circle. Ask, 'Who are you?'

You will get a sense of the answer, however your sensitivity is open to it, be it through sight or sound or sense.

Say what you feel. Is it a man? A woman? Are they young? Old? What are they saying to you? The important thing in any message is to identify the person communicating and to make sure that person is recognized by the recipient.

Don't go any further if they don't know who you are describing, no matter how rich the details may be. If you don't think the message is going to the right person, you cannot give it. So get the evidence you receive placed and make sure it is completely accepted.

Once your sitter has recognized the person coming through, ask that person why they are there. What's the reason behind it? And then they will give you the message. You can ask for more detail, too, but that's the basic idea.

It is also entirely acceptable to ask if there is anyone else in spirit who would like to give any messages to your sitter or to provide further evidence of their existence.

Keep the link as long as possible, so that the full message can be passed over. If the person's still there, don't stop! It's often doubt that stops you, and that's a reason to ... trust.

Trust, Trust, Trust
Trust the Process

When you first start as a medium, it is very easy to overemphasize the evidence and place that ahead of the message, but please, do not be tempted to do this. It is the message that you are there to deliver.

Likewise, do not keep asking the sitter for confirmation of all you are saying. By now you *know* you can link to spirit. Trust in that knowledge. Accept that whatever you receive – however bizarre! – it is for a good reason. Confirmation needs only to be established once, at the beginning, to identify the person communicating; any further will only confuse the reading and feed your ego!

Also, if you make that person think of all the practical details about who they've lost, that will only be painful and will help no one. This is why I believe that the message and the evidence are equally important.

When giving the message, try and make statements instead of asking questions and remember that the way you make those statements shows how confident you are. If you appear to know what you are doing, it will give the recipient confidence too.

Trust your Guide

As well as trusting in the process, you also have to trust in your spirit guide. There may be several spirits trying to come through at once – even someone trying to take their chance and shout something over the spirit guide. It can be mayhem, and if it is, you have to leave it up to your guide to sort it out.

You also have to trust your guide to bring through the evidence as quickly as possible. The best way to do this is to keep up the communication and ask for specific information. I'm always saying, 'Give me a date, give me a memory, give me a name.' That way you can get something definite that will make the person understand as quickly as possible who it is that's coming through. It's a lot quicker than spending a lot of time giving a description of the person.

In every situation, be aware of what you feel and sense, trust in it and act on it, no matter how strange the details may be. I once picked up a brand of children's aspirin, of all things, in a public demonstration, but when I mentioned it, a member of the audience could take it: he used to give it to his teenage daughter who had crossed.

McMessages

Healing someone's grief in a short time is quite a feat. You have to pinpoint the distress, address it and get the person to accept it and move on. It has to be very quick. So I give what I call 'MacMessages'. I've had amazing results with them. They've been magic that has really restored my faith in what I do.

The medium Mary Armour is also adept at these short messages. In one public demonstration I watched her as she pointed to a man at the back of the hall and said, 'Above your head I see the cartoon figure of Mickey Mouse, sir, and I hear the words, "Thank you."' The stunned man replied that he had paid for his nephew to go to Disneyland in Florida one month before he had died of cancer and said that that was all the proof he needed to know that his nephew was close to him.

Every one of us needs that magic from time to time. However long you've practised healing or mediumship, you'll still have moments of doubt. There'll be a morning when you'll wake up and think, 'Is it all real?' That's when you need to look for the magic again. You need to link with your higher self again. It's OK – it's just that you've lost the connection for a while.

'The Jewels of the Mind'

Grief is also a form of disconnection. It's not anger, it's loss and sadness. It's being cut off from the person who has died. One of the things that heals people's grief is reliving memories – happy memories of the times that they've spent with the person they've lost. Spirit often heals people through the use of memory. I'll pass on a message such as 'Your son says, "Do you remember when I was four and this happened?"' and see a mother's face light up.

These memories are what I call 'the jewels of the mind', the precious jewels that we've collected throughout our life. We store them in our mind and we can always replay them.

My own father has recently gone to the spirit world and I have been spending my time remembering how he taught me so many things as a child – simple things like how to tie my shoelaces or knot my school tie – and how he would sing to me if I couldn't sleep. It is so healing to remember the life that has gone in as many positive ways as you can.

So many people use the image of a person's death – or what they imagine happened when they died if they weren't there at the time – to torture themselves, rather than remembering that person's life and focusing on their *own* life. People see death as a punishment, particularly in the Western world, but it is actually part of life. It's perfectly natural. And if you accept that you're going to die, you can carry on with the business of living. Learning to accept death can actually bring us happiness. And healing – whether through a private reading or in another way – is all about making people happy.

Dealing with Emotional Pain

Sometimes contact will be made, but not with the loved one the recipient was expecting. This is often because it would be too emotionally painful for them to receive direct communication from that person at that time.

Also, you might pick up, say, that there has been a recent loss and it's a woman, but nothing more. A lot of the time that is nothing to do with the person in spirit not wanting to contact, but more because of the recipient's mindset. Even though they may think they want a message, they may not be ready to accept it, especially with a recent loss. Spirit will know if they are not ready for whatever reason, be it the circumstances of the loss, or the short period of time that has elapsed, or even because they are not ready to open their mind to the possibility of life continuing beyond physical death. Some people who come for private readings have already given that possibility a great deal of thought. Others have not, and to provide evidence of it, especially at such an emotional time, would be unkind to them. So spirit holds back.

I have had readings where the evidence has been incredibly accurate and the people that have come have been healed emotionally and gone away much lighter than they were. However, I have also had readings that were vague and cloudy and I received almost nothing from spirit.

The reason for this may be that if a person is stuck or confused or lost or hurt, to gain a message in this state would do more harm than good. People don't always know what they want when they are grieving: often the only thing that is certain is that they want their loved one back with them to hold. No one can provide this, and sometimes you can't connect with their spirit either.

If this happens, don't walk away feeling bad that you never got all the answers. Don't take personal responsibility for that. *It is not your fault.* As a medium, you just deliver messages. The lack of a message, especially this far in your development, will rarely be down to a lack of ability to receive. So, if you don't get a message, simply accept the possibility that the sitter is unready. Trust in spirit always.

With all this said, please, please learn to *enjoy* your work. Treat it, and the people who seek your help, with great respect and kindness, for this is the way of spirit, and bear in mind that the way you conduct yourself could govern the way people outside Spiritualist organizations perceive what you are doing. Simply take what is yours to give and share it sincerely, trusting those in spirit who guide you.

And above all else, to the best of your ability, remember kindness.

Practicalities

As well as all the emotional – and spiritual – side of things, there are some practicalities involved in giving private readings.

Recordings

Many clients request that the reading be recorded, so you may find it useful to purchase a dictaphone. However, over time I have found that the best readings, for whatever reason, are the ones that are not being recorded. This is not the same with every reading, but seems to be a general principle you might want to take into consideration.

It's All about Healing

Beyond any evidence you may give, ultimately your work as a medium is to *heal* through that evidence, using what you receive from spirit to help others, give comfort and enable them to carry on without the ones they loved.

I remember very clearly giving a reading to a couple whose child had died in a car crash. I was assuring them that their son was no longer in pain or suffering, when something occurred to me: that while their child had left long ago, the parents were still living the moment of the crash. Caught in the horror of losing their son, they felt unable to move forward. Was he hurt? Was he in pain? Is he still in pain? The answer to all three questions was 'no' – definitely no. In spirit no one has a physical body and so they cannot feel physical pain. However, it was clear that while the child wasn't in pain, his parents were. It was a great joy to be able to give them the reassurance they so needed to start the rest of their lives, free of guilt and remorse.

You will come across cases like this where people have suffered a tragic loss. But diving into their sea of emotions helps neither them nor you. You will doubtless be empathizing with what they are feeling and feeling compassion for them, but you are there, in whatever capacity, to pull them out of the emotional undercurrents rather than get sucked down yourself. Being positive is a big part of the healing you give.

Express your own Gratitude

A good way to remain positive is to express your gratitude. By doing this we say – to ourselves as much as anyone else – that we *do* have good things and good times in our lives and we are grateful for them.

Something that I do to keep positive is to say, when I wake up every day, 'Thank God, thank spirit and life, I have all these good things in my life.' I affirm to myself what I *have*, instead of what I haven't.

I cannot think of a healthier way to realize the love we can have for ourselves and the love that spirit gives us than to think positively.

It is also a good idea to stop from time to time and reflect on how our work as a medium has helped others. That, too, will keep our spirits up. In a manner of speaking!

Awareness of your Actions

Continuing with this, how we work relates to our awareness of our actions: how our lives will affect others. I look back karmically and think, 'My goodness, if my friend's brother had not died and not appeared to me, I would not be here now. From a death came my life.'

How many people does one death affect? How many people does one *life* affect? Understanding this, and working with that awareness, is part of what makes a good medium.

There are times when I've held a private reading and felt a shift in the energy of the people who have come for that reading. There have been times when the evidence I've provided has led to a considerable change in their attitude, belief and health. This is exactly why I work with spirit – to heal. But sometimes, that shift simply doesn't occur. If it doesn't, I don't beat myself up about it, and if you find yourself in this situation, I advise you not to either. So, please, if you feel that things have not gone well, don't feel guilty, or try to assign blame anywhere. You have done what you can. You may even have sown seeds that will bear fruit in the future. But for now you must leave it there.

Reflection

Finally, it's always a good idea to reflect on each private reading you give as a medium. Consider why it went the way it did and how you can improve next time. Reflect on the energies that you felt and how or if they changed. This will help you with future readings.

11
Platform Work

'Each cell in my body has divine intelligence.
I listen to what it tells me and know that
its advice is valid.'
LOUISE L. HAY

First attempts at mediumship in front of a public gathering can be among the most nerve-wracking times in your life. Even though you have practised forging a link with your spirit guides and helpers for many years, nothing prepares you for your first encounter with the general public. Everything you have learned in development seems to go out of the window!

First-Night Nerves

One night whilst driving to my Spiritualist church to attend a service of mediumship, I became aware of a feeling of intensity growing somewhere within me. I was nervous and afraid, yet of what? I had no reason to be scared.

The only thing I knew was that at times in the past when this feeling had occurred, something important had been about to happen to me or to someone close to me. That was as much as I could be sure of, only this time I couldn't think what to expect. One thing I did know: I wasn't going to be working on the platform that night as a medium. Not in a million years.

And yet, as it happened, that Sunday evening our medium hadn't turned up to take the service. No other medium could be found within the congregation, so the gentleman chairing the meeting, who was not mediumistic himself, decided that I should go on.

If this kind of surprise debut ever happens to any of you as developing mediums, I can tell you it has the most humbling effect on you that you could ever imagine.

I can remember sending out so many prayers, pleading with God and all the spirit helpers I had ever known in the desperate hope that the absent medium would turn up just in time to save me. When I realized that I would have to go on with this particular 'show' and that there was no turning back, I began to plead with God again, more urgently this time, pledging with all of my soul that I would become a really good person *if this could just work.*

There is nothing I can tell you about coping with this type of situation that will really give you much in the way of help, except that you must trust in the spirit friends with whom you have bonded throughout your early development. It is exactly this type of unanticipated test that will prove to you that you *do* have what it takes to continue your journey and to persevere with your work as a medium in this fashion.

Somehow, I managed to get through that particular evening, although, I must say, somewhat overwhelmed and overshadowed. The relief I felt when the chairperson called me to time was so great that I wanted to laugh out loud.

To this day I don't really remember the finer points of the demonstration; it seemed to have flown by before I realized it, but I had finally taken my first step as a public demonstrator of mediumship. And it felt incredibly humbling and deeply inspiring at the same time. I realized this was but a glimpse of what I could achieve on the platform if I continued to put a lot of work and dedication into it.

Trial Runs

If it is your good fortune to be allowed to practise public demonstrating within a group, seminar or workshop where people around you understand your inexperience and lend you their support, you are less likely to come unstuck if thrown onto the platform in an impromptu situation as I was.

It would be my advice to all students with the gift of mediumship who wish to venture forth into public platform work to have as many 'trial runs' or 'fledgling evenings' as possible. Most Spiritualist churches and organizations will schedule such events for the pupils who sit in their circles and their groups.

Be Sure You're Ready to Face the Public

Please do not be over-keen to demonstrate your gift in the early days, particularly in public. There are several reasons for this. First, one thing you are not taught how to develop in your group is a 'thick skin' – and believe me, you will need it! I was very lucky that the spirit world overshadowed me on my first outing and literally took over the demonstration by using me as their medium in a semi-state of trance. It could well have been a rougher ride.

How you fare on your first outing can often determine how much you will achieve if you decide to stay the course, so take care in accepting that first invitation. Remember, the general public who attend such meetings have a whole host of different needs. Many will be filled with deep sorrows or grief and of course some will come along just to give you a hard time. Not everyone sitting within a Spiritualist congregation will be sympathetic towards you. Some of the responses you receive will be most off-putting! Still, aim to deliver your messages with confidence. The tone of your voice will have an impact on all those hearing you.

What you learn in terms of handling different situations with compassion and grace in your early days as a platform medium visiting small Spiritualist churches will become invaluable to you as you progress further and travel more widely. This is why I believe wholeheartedly that student mediums should spend as much time as necessary practising within the safety of their groups to build up their confidence before facing the general public.

I had no confidence when I first started to speak on a public platform – even the thought terrified me. Now I can manage three hours and be happy. The difference that has come about through practice and reflection is enormous. I have learned to conquer my fear through believing that if you have a message that needs to be given, you *have* to get up and talk. Fear is only ego – in this case, it is fear of looking silly or being wrong. But be brave: the message is more important than your nerves!

And with all that has happened to me, I am still the same person I was in that I still ask spirit with all my heart to help me every time I go on a public platform. I always ask permission from them: 'Is it right to help this person? May I be used as the instrument to serve you?'

What's for You Won't Go by You

As I mentioned at the start of this book, I know it to be true that anyone who is *meant* to do this work will find a way. If you are meant to be on a public platform, the chance will not pass you by. If at first you miss it, another chance will appear. And another. So keep your heart open, your intentions clear and your confidence up. You will know when the time is right for you.

Life on the Road

Working with spirit has given me some wonderful opportunities to travel that I am extremely grateful for. It is a great privilege to be on the road if you are called to do so, and it is also a good test of your mediumship skills. When you are away from your usual platform, you know for a fact that there is nothing you can know about the people who are attending.

Speaking in Tongues

This is especially true in countries where the language is different and you need to talk through an interpreter. When I have been working through an interpreter, I have found it really reassuring that sometimes I will pick up information in other languages – something I always find amazing, as I have no knowledge of any other language than English.

I remember one time when I was in Germany and I was mid-message with an interpreter who was taking too long. I had a six-year-old girl who was communicating with her mother in the audience and I knew the interpreter was saying more than was required. As the minutes were ticking by, I was becoming more and more frustrated by how long it was taking. Finally I just thought in exasperation, 'Oh, just use me, spirit!' and I felt that little girl come through me and speak directly to her mother – in German.

The interpreter stopped mid-flow – everyone in the room was shocked! But the young girl calmly carried on through me, thanking her mother for everything she had done and saying that she knew her mother believed in angels and now she herself was an angel. She even said she was glad she had been to Australia! Of course I knew nothing about any of this – I just stood by and let the words pour out of my mouth. Then it stopped as suddenly as it had begun and I could no more speak German after that than fly.

It occurred to me afterwards, reflecting on my frustration, that spirit communicators might feel something similar when working through mediums. With interpreters, in a sense you are acting in the same way: you are reliant on the person translating what you know and have to hope it will get communicated properly. There was a great deal to be learned from that and one of those lessons, for me, was how to become more concise and correct about what I was trying to relate through an interpreter.

It's all about getting the message across.

Beware of Hubris

Working in public gives an enormous source of energy because of all the people sending out thoughts and wishes for a message. Suddenly you find yourself looked up to by an entire congregation of hopeful souls, and if you are good, it is so easy to forget the very reason for your quick fame. Rather than focusing on helping others, you can bask in their adulation. The public platform is occasionally the place where a medium's ego can be polished to such an extent that they forget why they began their development course in the first place.

Should ego ever arise because of your success as a medium, then recognize it *quickly* and deal with it accordingly. Hubris can be your greatest downfall as a medium. Remember, you are simply the postman, delivering messages of guidance, comfort and love. You are *not* the creator of those messages. That task belongs to the higher spirit world.

Typical Platform

I seemed to do a big part of my public platform development 'on the run' as it were, learning as I went along, accepting the mistakes I made and forgiving myself for them as well. It was often tough and uncharted terrain, but I made progress.

If I were to try to describe to you what it feels like to give a service of mediumship from start to finish, it would be something a little like this. The moment I arrive on the platform is the point at which I begin to send out my signal to my spirit communicators, tuning in and asking them to help direct the coming service. My mind becomes more and more focused on the spirits around me rather than on what is happening in the room or what my chairperson is saying to the congregation.

From this moment forward, I am totally open to the spirit world. If a prayer or public address is required at the start, then I have to trust in my spirit controls to guide the essence, tone or philosophy of the message so that it touches as many hearts in the gathering as possible.

I have often worked with mediums who say that before coming to a service, even a day or two before demonstrating, they will receive specific messages from people in the spirit world which they are to offer out to the congregation. This never seems to happen to me. Well, hardly ever, if at all. At least I am never aware of it happening ahead of the scheduled meeting time. My understanding of how public mediumship works is that we link in to the energies present at a particular moment in place and time as and when we first begin to work. For me, that moment is when I first step onto the platform.

Once the chairperson invites me to demonstrate, I mentally ask the spirit people if they would like to communicate. From that moment on, everything becomes spontaneous for me. It feels as if there is an overshadowing of my own being as my spirit control moves closer and takes over. This is why it is difficult to explain the proper mechanics of a clairvoyant demonstration to those who ask you questions about the type of mediumship you have just demonstrated.

Ways of Working

I don't actually believe mediums should become overly concerned with terms like 'clairvoyance' or 'clairaudience', 'clairsentience' or even 'trance'. Whatever is meant to come through comes, no matter what form is favoured by spirit at the moment. To label a form of mediumship is automatically to limit it. You never know beforehand how a particular message will be delivered. You simply link with your guide and helpers and leave the work to them. It is best to just get out of the way and let spirit use as much of the human space as possible. Let go and trust. Take this notion to heart.

Even though the general public may not be aware of the slight state of trance you may be in while working on the podium, good mediumship will always involve some form of overshadowing. For a number of years now I have been aware that Chi, the spirit who controls the part of my work that involves clairvoyance, has been responsible for all of the seeing, hearing and sensing of the spirit people wishing to communicate with their loved ones. So even though I and other mediums may state that 'we' see or hear a spirit, actually it is the working or controlling spirit, in my case Chi, who passes the information to us via the link we have made with them.

As soon as the demonstration is over, my link with the spirit world closes down and I quickly 'switch off' – that crucial discipline learned early in development circle.

In trying to describe the sensation for you, I would say that it is not as though I have been in a deep trance, but rather as if my own thoughts have been completely bypassed by the thoughts of those in spirit who have been working through me. It's a little bit like waking up from a daydream, but within seconds my own conscious mind is reconnected. I don't mean to suggest that I have been unaware of the proceedings, but rather that spirit has had the freedom of my thought processes and my imagination.

At the end of a service, if it has flowed continuously, with many clear messages being delivered, then the medium should experience an overall sense of tranquillity and well-being. On the other hand, if during the demonstration the medium has lost the link with spirit on several occasions and dropped down to the psychic level to supplement the energies from their own reserves, then they may feel a physical and/or mental tiredness. It is through these effects that we can often register how much work we have carried out on the spirit level and how much, if any, on the psychic plane. In either case, it's then time to go off and ground ourselves by living our lives.

Remember Kindness

If you find it is your path to demonstrate public mediumship, then try always to be sincere in what you do and the way in which you do it. Remember that most of the people you see will be hurting inside, however strong and composed they may appear on the outside. Be kind and let spirit do the rest.

12
Tough Trade

*'As a medium, if you take praise from the public,
be sure there will be criticism to follow.'*
ALBERT BEST

There are many different ways of working professionally
as a medium and how you offer your services is
entirely down to what *you* are comfortable with. You can
rely on word of mouth. You can advertise your services
through newspapers, magazines or the internet. You can
travel. You can stay where you trained. It is up to you.
Go where you are called, wherever that may be.

How you work can be just as varied as where you work.
Remember you have the ability and freedom to change any
circumstances that do not suit you or feel right at any time.

Starting Out

If you consider mediumship as your work, then embarking
on work with the public is no different from any other

new job you might begin. The circle, and all of its careful preparations, reminded me of my time at hairdressing college, when absolutely everything I did was supervised by my teacher. It was a world unto itself and the people I practised on knew that I was a full-fledged novice.

Then, out of the blue, that big leap comes along. Suddenly someone's sitting in your chair, a real live customer, and you've got to 'perform'. The first day I was promoted to do actual salon work for the paying public, I was so terrified of making mistakes and messing things up that I just stood about like an apprentice, looking clumsy and getting in the way. I nearly lost that job. Inside my head I knew exactly how to put into practice all of the skills I had learned and practised at college, yet somehow I couldn't bring them to my fingertips in this strange pressurized environment.

Your first few practices as a medium can be quite similar. Before demonstrating, you believe yourself to be fully prepared and in your head you can hear yourself tuning in, the way you always do in circle. You begin to feel the presence of the spirit people around you and everything feels very much on track. You begin to relax, knowing that they are there to support you in every way.

Then, when the voice of the chairperson announces you are about to give a demonstration of clairvoyance, everything just goes, vanishes, just like that, and there's not enough time to tune in again. You start to pray furiously inside your own head. You can't remember any of the helpful hints you learned in development. People are looking at you, waiting expectantly for you to speak and hoping that you will bring messages to them from their loved ones on the other side. For a moment you panic, feeling that absolutely nothing is going to happen...

Recovery Routine

What should you do when this occurs? I can only share with you what I do; in time, you will develop your own recovery routine.

I have a standard practice when this type of incident happens: I take a deep breath and a small drink of water and I speak to the congregation. I am always honest with them and I just talk to them from the heart. The worst thing you can ever do is to attempt to give messages when in reality nothing is coming through. You will make matters worse by trying to drag spirit information through a mind that has become tense and narrow.

So take a moment to compose yourself and to tell the people whom you are addressing how you are feeling. There is nothing like honesty to open up your mind.

This will allow the spirit controls who are working with you to make a stronger link so that you can continue.

Remember, you are not on trial! You are there to share a gift.

What If You Don't Get a Message?

Whether you are giving private readings or doing platform work, never be ashamed to admit to people if nothing is coming through to you from the spirit world. Just be kind and be truthful. Have the courage to say, 'I'm sorry, there isn't a strong connection. I'm not getting anything through.' Most people will understand this.

As I mentioned before, some people are just not ready to receive a message and the spirit world will know that. Other people will come to see a medium when they don't really need to and there's no message there for them. In either case, stop trying to get one, because this can be psychically draining for you.

What If They Become Angry?

Be aware, however, that whether you have a message to deliver or not, there will be times when the recipient will be angry. I have had readings several times in my life where people have ranted and raved at me – some of them even becoming angry at the very beginning, before I've really said anything.

When this happens – and sooner or later it will – try and keep your perspective and understand that these people wouldn't be so angry unless something important was happening to them. You have to keep in mind that mediumship is a form of therapy for bereavement and that no one who comes to you will be that angry unless they have been hurt, or are afraid, or are going through something very difficult for them.

There is always the chance that their anger may in fact be a defence mechanism in case you get a message: anger is another demonstration of how people may not be ready for a message or any evidence of spirit.

Above all, *don't retaliate*. As a medium you don't just have to be incredibly sensitive to those in spirit but also to the people who have come to you for a reading. If they are angry or show their frustration, then that is when you need to care *more* about them. Talk to them. If necessary, stop the reading. Wind it down. Say something like, 'I'm sorry you're angry and we've had to stop. Maybe it's not the right time for you to have a reading now.' Give the best advice you can and be honest but kind.

One example of this was a lady who came to the church I was at with her husband for a reading. I made a connection very easily, and in terms of evidence, spirit was able to give her a lot. She had lost a son in his twenties. He came through and explained that he had died recently in hospital of an illness and had left a child behind. He was even able to give the song that had been played at his funeral. The message that he wanted to give was even clearer: his parents were fighting a custody battle for his child – their grandchild – with the child's mother, who wouldn't let them visit. Because of this they were starting legal action to adopt his son. However, he was desperate for them not to continue with it.

All through this there were little chips of evidence flying in all directions: something his father had in his pocket, items his parents had deliberately brought with them but hadn't taken out of their bags, things they had spoken to him about that very day.

After about half an hour, when I finished delivering the message, the woman said tersely, 'I'm not buying this. I'm not convinced.'

Her husband was very surprised. 'But how could he know these things?'

She grew extremely angry and replied, 'He never told me my son's middle name!'

It would have been very easy for me for to bite back, even with a sarcastic reply, but I didn't. Instead I looked at her and saw how sad she was and thought, 'You poor woman – all that evidence and you just wanted me to say his middle name?' I hadn't even thought to ask; I don't have a middle name myself and it hadn't occurred to me that that was the one piece of evidence she felt she needed.

I bit my tongue, kept calm and said I was sorry she was so angry but that was the message I had received.

Still she could not accept it and left. I was a little saddened, but felt there was nothing more I could do to help.

Six weeks later, I received a letter from her and her husband, thanking me. After a lot of careful thought they had realized their son had been right and they had taken his advice: they had chosen not to pursue the legal action and instead were focusing on forming a relationship with their grandson and his mother. Already they were much happier and there was some hope for the future.

The truth was that their custody battle had simply been an outlet for their pain. The woman in particular had needed to blame *someone* for her loss, even though it had been nobody's fault. Both parents had been frightened and desperate not to lose anything else to do with their son, and they had felt the only way was to battle for custody.

I realized that there was a lesson in this: that there is a clear difference between what someone *wants* and what someone *needs*. The message that couple had received had been something they hadn't *wanted* to hear at all, but accepting the evidence that their son was still alive in spirit and choosing to forgive and love rather than take possession of their grandson had brought the healing they *needed*.

What those left behind receive is sometimes not what they expect, and they have to deal with that. But that doesn't mean that you should ever allow them to become abusive towards you.

What If They Don't Accept the Message?

One of the most frustrating things I found during my early work was the number of times I would pass information to a sitter and they would not understand it or would steadfastly refuse to accept it. This is even more frustrating in a public forum, when you *know* that you have been given strong evidence from the spirit world specifically for a person and all they say is, 'No, no, no!' Not only can this type of response shatter your confidence as a medium, but it can also cause the gathering to question your gift or your sincerity and the energies in the whole room to drop.

The more advanced practitioners of mediumship seem to be able to cope with these situations easily and well, without losing their link to spirit or their belief in what is being communicated. But the novice sometimes appears like a young salmon swimming upstream, becoming twisted and tangled in a net and struggling furiously to shake free. It is this struggle that causes the exhaustion of everyone's energies. Other people then become uncomfortable and a palpable awkwardness can be felt all around.

It is not a happy place to be. However, the one thing you must not do is to confront anyone or try to force a message onto them.

How do you resolve this sort of stalemate?

First of all, end the struggle immediately. Offer the information kindly and compassionately to the recipient if you are definite that it is for them; then, if rebuffed, ask them to please hold the information until a later date, when what you have relayed to them may make more sense or they may have a chance to check it over with someone else in their family or circle of friends. Whatever you do, don't make it into a battle. There are no winners or losers in this kind of privileged exchange.

Naturally, any form of mediumship works better if there is harmony. But your job is only to give evidence to establish the links, then to deliver the messages offered, after which the recipient must decide how much of it applies to them. You need pass no judgement on their replies. Simply offer up what you have to share and ask in your heart that the highest good be served in their receiving the messages intended for them to hear.

Even if the messages are accurate, some people will dismiss what you are saying by claiming that you're 'just' reading minds. 'Oh, he's not getting messages from spirits, he's just telepathic!' Hang on, what's that all about? Wouldn't that be amazing? That would in itself be an extension of the human mind that we haven't yet tapped into. But for some people it's just an excuse not to believe what you say because, for whatever reason, they're not ready to take on board all the implications.

Other people will claim almost defiantly not to know what you are giving them. If this happens, don't lose heart. I've delivered so many messages from the platform that people wouldn't accept at the time and then later, upon checking with loved ones, realized were relevant. If every working medium had a pound for every time a message wasn't understood at the moment it was delivered but was later found to be correct, we'd all be very rich!

So many times people write to me after private readings saying that there was something they didn't accept but on arriving home they found something that showed that it was right after all.

On one occasion, while making a pilot for a TV programme, I was asked to give messages to the audience as part of the film. The first message that came through was from a lady's father in the spirit world. She accepted everything I told her but for one thing: he mentioned an old picture of him with a friend called Alec, who had been in the navy with him in his youth, and she was adamant that he hadn't known anyone of that name.

When the filming was over, one of the researchers from the film crew went home with the lady to collect footage of the items that had been mentioned in the message and to film her reaction post-message. They were all shocked when, while looking for the other pictures I had told her about, she came across a photo of two young sailors and on the back were the words, in her father's hand, 'Me and Alec'.

Again, that little word 'trust' comes into play. *The sacred rule of mediumship is to give what you get, then let it be.* Don't start doubting yourself, otherwise you will start to lose the link with spirit and then you will make mistakes. So, once again, *trust.*

What If They Hero Worship You?

You may laugh, but over time you will encounter people who mistakenly believe that you have access to a limitless fount of knowledge. Actually, spirit *is* limitless in terms of knowledge, but your access to it is not. Be clear with people: *what you receive is entirely down to what spirit chooses to give you.* This is not to say the details are like pick 'n' mix, but you have little or no control over what you receive. Connecting with spirit, particularly with mediumship, is not like connecting with a search engine on the internet: you cannot look for what somebody wants. You can only be open to what is sent to you.

A good way to avoid any hero worship – and there really is a chance of it happening, especially when someone is troubled emotionally – is to behave appropriately both inside and outside a reading and in your everyday life.

Also, your work with spirit does not need to be advertised 24 hours a day, seven days a week. While certainly you shouldn't hide who you are and what you do, by continually talking about mediumship and how wonderful it is, you stand a chance of instilling false expectations and hopes in others. Remember, you are an ambassador for the spirit world, so behave accordingly. You don't need to show off, or flaunt what you know. That should be reserved for those who need it. For example, if someone says to you, 'Can you tell me what's going to happen tomorrow?', it's a clear sign that they're curious but not in need of any help. With people like these, by all means be amiable, but do not engage further. You don't need to tune in to spirit for people who ask frivolous questions – you risk wasting your time and energy.

This is especially important to remember if you are just starting out as a medium, as you will be asked a lot of questions that you may not be sure how to respond to and may get quite a few requests. The simplest way is always to be honest about what you can and can't do. Just relax, be friendly and smile. Clear up misconceptions, but do no more. You are responsible for your own space, so have the courage to keep people from invading it – or putting you on a pedestal.

Those who are close to you are often very good at keeping you from getting above yourself. My mother and father, very down-to-earth people, just called mediumship 'that thing that you do'. Before she came to see me on a platform, my mother had no idea of what it really entailed and even told people I was singing in a choir in Belgium once, but, as she said, it was OK because she knew it was holy...

A Process of Growth

Growth comes from experiencing both good times and more difficult ones, and the more difficult parts of our spiritual journey can also keep our spiritual ego in check. Spiritual ego can be the most difficult form of ego to detect. However, mediums can be brought back down to earth quite swiftly. Any of us can have an off night, because we're all human.

At difficult times, remember that you're there to deliver a message and you can do no more. And you're always learning and improving.

Dealing with People's Fears

When people do talk to you about mediumship, you have the power to give another perspective, one that could allay some of their fears. In truth, the majority of people love to feel scared. However, there comes a point when that fear runs out of their control, and this is very easy with matters of spirit and physical death.

Ghosts and Hauntings

A few times members of the public have approached me to talk about ghosts and hauntings – terrified members of the public at that. When this happens, it is a very good opportunity to reassure any fears by applying your own experience.

For example, I remember one time when a woman approached me to talk about a local haunting of a child who had died.

'It's as if they're stuck between worlds,' she said.

The truth of this is that spirits on the earth plane are very rare. Nothing can stop a spirit from moving into the spirit world. It doesn't matter whether suicide or murder or some other form of trauma is associated with its passing, it will still move on. What might be left behind are memories – traumatic memories. Psychics and mediums who do what is known as 'rescue work' are cleaning up the stains, if you like, that a human life has left behind it. That's why this work can be traumatic – because they're the memories of traumatic events.

In fact, we all leave our own memories lying about in our own homes – a good psychic can pick up on what has happened to the people living in a house just by walking into it. The same principle comes into play with psychometry, where psychics read the emotional memories left behind in an object that has belonged to someone. What we perceive as ghosts and hauntings are similar emotional imprints. They can be triggered when certain people arrive in a place. People who are sensitive or psychic or frightened can bring those memories back to the fore. They may start to download them and believe them to be real, but they aren't real, they're just memories.

With all this in mind, I was naturally uncomfortable with the view that the child's spirit was stuck between worlds. When I was able to explain that this was highly unlikely to be the case, the woman was reassured.

As a medium, you may be called upon to go and help people who believe they are being haunted. I've seen so many so-called possessions and hauntings. Before you get to a place, you will hear all sorts of horrors about it. 'There's a cold chill in the room,' people will say. There's an easy answer to this: close the window! You would be amazed at how often basic common sense has gone out of that window in these cases, but it's because people's fears have got a hold on them and so they aren't thinking sensibly.

Moreover, when someone's frightened they can make anything happen. They create it. And then that disturbs them even more and it becomes a self-perpetuating cycle of fear. Our mind can actually work for us in a very negative way if we're full of fear, and that's what so often happens with hauntings: people's own fears are magnified and reflected back to them. Sometimes they can be possessed by their own fears.

Even when the 'haunting' is not down to people's fears or an emotional imprint they've picked up and there is something of a 'paranormal' nature there, it's often someone in the spirit world trying to get someone's attention for one reason or another. But people who are not used to the unseen world will project their own fear onto that. It's all too easy if you don't have any experience of other worlds and/or believe that this is all there is. So have compassion for these people – in some cases they may be consciously crying out for attention, but in most instances they are genuinely afraid and unaware of how to deal with what's happening to them.

If you are invited along to a house to see 'paranormal phenomena' for yourself, it's always good to take someone with you who's sensible. It helps to restore a sense of normality and reassure the person who is afraid, and it is better that two people are there to validate what, if anything, is actually happening. I always take someone with me.

One time, I remember, I went with Tricia Robertson from the Scottish Society for Psychical Research to a home in Scotland where two teenage girls were terrified to sleep in one of the bedrooms. After some sensible questioning by Tricia and not that much tuning in by me, we discovered that their grandfather had died in the room several months before and that all they were afraid of was actually coming from their own heads. Still, we had to reassure them, and I went into the room, tuned in and got a lovely message from the deceased man telling them that there was nothing to fear and that he did not dwell there, nor had he ever frightened them – it was just their imagination.

If you are ever asked to investigate a similar case, if you go along without fear and with a genuine desire to help the people who are being disturbed in one way or another, you will soon be able to sort things out and leave them free to get on with their lives rather than being hampered by fear.

Tips for the Fledgling Medium

It's one thing to be doing well in your development circle and realizing that your mediumship is coming on in leaps and bounds. It is a very different thing when it comes to working with the general public away from the safety of the friendship and spiritual power of your circle.

• Remember, you will have good and bad days when you work as a medium. Some demonstrations or one-to-ones will be very accurate and satisfying for both you and the recipient. But accept both good and bad as learning experiences and never forget that you are not 100 per cent yet – or possibly ever, because we're all human.

- Don't think that because you are working as a medium you have 'arrived'. You can still develop much more; so keep attending your circle for as long as you can. You have never finished learning.

- Treat every one-to-one or public demonstration as the first. Don't think that because you have been successful in past work you can become complacent.

- Remember that the people who seek your gift do so because they need help. But never try to categorize grief or human suffering. You are a messenger, not a judge.

- Always, always practise your gift with the intention of helping people. Never perform just to appear clever or different from others.

- Never start any practice of mediumship or healing without first asking spirit for permission. Their presence is what fuels your work. Their absence would tell you that it is not appropriate to work. And, it's only courtesy to thank them when you finish.

- Never be afraid to ask spirit to help you when you are stuck with something. Even in mid-message it is OK to mentally check in with them and ask for things to be given again for clarity.

- In all spiritual practices, remember kindness.

13
Learning and Teaching

*'The possibility of stepping into a higher plane is
quite real for everyone. It requires no force or effort
or sacrifice. It involves little more than changing
our ideas about what is normal.'*

DEEPAK CHOPRA

As time has passed I have found that as I develop my
own skills, I am both able and willing to teach. I feel
very blessed to be able to share my experiences through
workshops and books and to introduce others to spirit.
It may well be that at some point in your life as a medium
you will be able to do the same. With this in mind, I would
like to give you advice that I hope will help you when you
start out as a teacher.

One of the first things is to listen to every single
student. Each student is an individual, with different skills,
needs and desires, and it pays to always keep this in mind.
Listen to what they have to say and find out why they want
to develop. As I have said before, a new class of developing

mediums is a lot like a class of children: you need to identify their traits, loves and habits, and work with them to iron out their faults, just as your teacher did with you.

Ultimately, as a teacher of mediums you must display patience. You will hopefully have learned it through your own development! The pupils you take on will be at different levels and have different fears and abilities. You will have students who will sit down and be rational about their experiences, students who will be bursting with eagerness to describe what they have seen and felt with life and colour and passion, and also students who will be easily frightened and may have experienced grievous emotional hurt in their lives. These are the ones who need the most attention; however, part of your skill as a teacher is to ensure every pupil feels that they are getting enough guidance in their development.

You will also need to create a balance in the group. Those students who are quiet and appear lifeless will need to be lifted, just as those who are excitable will need to be calmed down. As a teacher, you are essentially linking energy to energy through finding that balance, in order to create an equality for every member of the group that in turn will help forge a stable connection with spirit.

Awareness and Intention

The whole process needs to be slow and correct in order to help everyone adjust rather than just a few. Some pupils may show great aptitude in one area, but you cannot marvel at that – as a teacher, you must always pull on the reins. It is easy to let someone go public too quickly; they may appear ready, but are often not, for a variety of reasons. No matter how accurate they are at giving messages, you must always remember that they are not just learning about delivering but about themselves too.

My own focus when teaching is always on self-awareness: examining ourselves and how and why we are acting the way we are. I have to ascertain each student's reasons for developing and whether the pace they are setting for themselves is right for them or if they are at risk of burnout. Do they think it is going to be a lifelong process or just a fad? How do they intend to use the abilities they develop?

I remember one young man who came into my circle to work with us. At the age of 19 he was already a fantastic medium: his messages were incredibly detailed, he was almost never wrong, and the evidence was clear, unambiguous and accurate. However, he was so young that he had hardly done anything in his life apart from give messages. I remember saying to him, 'You need to get some life experience, because the way you rattle your messages out, there is no compassion.'

The problem was that he didn't appear to understand the impact of the messages he received and above all *how* he gave them. So he'd be talking to people and saying, 'You've lost a son, and this is his name, but you need to get over it,' all in one breath. When delivering, you simply cannot be so blunt. The impact those messages can have on those receiving them can be immense. So the *way* you deliver a message can be just as important as the message itself. This requires compassion and is perfected through experience.

With this young man, there was simply no tact nor diplomacy because he had never encountered any deep emotional experiences himself. He could take the evidence, but he could not connect with the level of emotion or hurt that he was dealing with.

'You need to sit in circle,' I told him. 'You need to develop.'

However, he didn't listen. Instead, he focused his efforts on getting accurate messages.

Within two years, he had totally given up mediumship. He had burnt out; he was disillusioned and he didn't understand why he was doing it. He saw no point to it. Because he had no real knowledge or experience of any aspect of mediumship other than the accuracy of the message, he couldn't relate to any of the emotional relief he had brought to people. Also, as a result of focusing on the evidence, whenever someone told him, 'No, that's not right,' he took it very personally. He couldn't handle it, because he had no inner strength. And so he stopped mediumship – he crashed and burned.

Reality Checks

When working as a medium or teaching others, always have reality checks. Always examine and reflect and realize when you need to head back into circle and learn more, or indeed unlearn any bad habits that you have picked up on the road.

Every medium, no matter how far or successful they get, encounters times when they need to head back into circle, to go back into the spiritual classroom to take another course. There will come times when you need to add to your existing experience in a deeper sense, one that is closer to spirit than continually working on a platform or holding private readings or healing the public, and circle will provide just that.

Development is what sustains my mediumship and I feel this is a universal truth for all mediums. I recently joined my old friends from my first private circle again after an absence of a few years, and the feeling of joining together again was like coming home. The reconnection of not just a circle but the members' guides feels like old friends reuniting; there is a safety in it, a welcoming and warmth and familiarity that feel much like the first time you connect with spirit. No one will ever say you can't go back into circle, sometimes with old members, sometimes welcoming and teaching new members too.

In fact, development never ends, because what you have done up until this point could all change tomorrow when you encounter somebody else. Giving them a message could enhance your understanding. So even with a great deal of experience, never think you have reached your peak. Each situation will be new, and that is what keeps your mediumship fresh and worth doing. Every day is a day where new people are hurting, new people need understanding.

One of my favourite aspects about teaching is that the students you encounter very often teach you. The situations and emotional hurdles that they have to overcome can be very different from those you have experienced. If I've learned anything about development, it's that teaching and being taught are the most exciting parts of it.

You must also look for what spirit is trying to bring forward by way of teaching. Ultimately, if you are teaching mediumship, you are being taught to teach by spirit. You are learning as much as you would if you were in circle. There is always a teacher above you. Therefore it can be quite humbling when you teach people about spirit. You soon realize that you are not the be-all and end-all because the public have deemed you to be good. The ultimate teachers, and also assessors of your work, come from the spirit world.

The Philosophy of Spirit

When I first heard a spirit control speaking through his entranced medium, I was truly overwhelmed. The medium later became a good friend, as, I suppose, did the control. The content of that particular discussion was the spiritual evolution of humankind and how we have lost our spiritual awareness, blinded by the explosion of materialism and concentration on that which can be seen, heard, touched and purchased.

The talk must have gone on for some 30 minutes or so, yet upon reflection the whole thing could have been expressed in one minute – or at least that's how it felt to me. I remember clearly being absolutely compelled to attend the address and being enchanted by the choice of words and the gentle calming sound of the spirit voice that held the small audience of six completely spellbound.

That voice seemed to be accompanied by an inexplicable warmth that somehow wrapped itself around us, giving a feeling of utter protection and comfort. It was explained to us that we should try to not only sense but also understand the *vibration* of sound being given off by the spirit rather than envisaging a picture relating to the spoken word. What this meant was that we should try to open up to the sound, rather than to the specific suggestion. By opening our minds to this form of communication, we would be expanding our awareness of spirit, rather than falling back on our own preconceived ideas.

Whenever spirit chooses to use a medium in trance, it is to simplify what it is trying to teach us. By using the entranced medium's body and voice, the spirit control can impart a more direct lesson. However, by teaching us in this way, the spirits are as limited as we are, for they will come up against the same sorts of restrictions that any teacher or philosopher will find in being restricted to the use of material words to try to describe spiritual experiences.

Spiritual experiences are always diluted by the symbolism we require to interpret what we cannot understand of the higher worlds around us. This is why when you are fortunate enough to be allowed to experience the trance teachings of an enlightened spirit teacher, you must open up your heart and listen with your entire being to all that is being expressed. Allow your consciousness to grow because of it. It is only when you can appreciate the entire experience that it will raise your own consciousness to a new level of understanding. Otherwise, you would do just as well to refer to books on the subject. Once again, I bring you back to the simple fact that spirit speaks to us through our senses.

The Truth Can Hurt

More often than I would care to remember, however, I have listened to so-called mediums in so-called trance delivering so-called spiritual addresses to groups of people gathered to hear what they hope will be the truth of spirit, only to be disappointed time and time again. What they get instead is a set of platitudes that cover everything from birth to death, with a bit of drama sprinkled throughout.

The more evolved spirit people who do happen to shine through on these occasions seem to speak more of compassion, so inevitably stand out. Remembering that compassion is a double-edged sword, not everything that is said by these higher beings is beautiful and pleasant. But then you have to ask yourself whether it's likely to be the truth.

I suppose what I'm trying to point out is this: don't get swept away by teachings that paint pictures of an artificially beautiful life and a wonderful saccharine existence. Remember, life *can* be tough. And most honest teachers will prepare us for the truth of this wisdom by pointing out the pitfalls of life as well as reminding us of its natural beauties.

All You Need...

And yet in the end it's all very simple. One of the most precious pieces of philosophy I was ever given by spirit was this: 'Learn to love each other.'

It may appear obvious, but once we have absorbed the sentiment with a heightened awareness, it seems to be all we need to guide us spiritually in this world.

Afterword

*'Spiritualism has been to me, in common with
others, such a lifting of the mental horizon
and letting in of the heavens.'*
GERALD MASSEY

In my own experience as a medium, I must admit there
have been days when, despite my best intentions and
all of the steps I have taken along the path, I could have
thrown in the proverbial towel. But something always kept
me going. Someone always seemed to be in the right place
at the right time to lend encouragement for me to continue.
For that, I am extremely grateful and glad.

As a medium, there will also be times, as I have
mentioned briefly before, when friends and even loved
ones will not or simply cannot understand what it is that
compels you to carry on. They may even try to dissuade
you from continuing, either because they fear that they are
somehow 'losing' you to this other world, or, even scarier
to them, fear you may leave them behind. As you have
discovered on your journey, fear is a great limiter. As such,

it falls on you to help others understand how and why your gift is being developed and used, and to reassure them that this in no way excludes them or makes them less important in your everyday life. This is not always easy, but is well worth the effort. There is nothing that says you have to sacrifice all those you love and cherish in order to become a good medium.

Despite the occasional moments of doubt, as a result of my extensive time in development – which continues to this day – I have gained a faith that I'm sure could move mountains if necessary, and hopefully enough compassion to last a lifetime of bringing comfort and upliftment to all those I can. Even more than all of this, I personally have found an invaluable freedom to express my understanding of life, both here and beyond, to any and all who are willing to listen.

To anyone who is interested in developing their awareness of this life and the life still to come, either as a medium or in some other capacity, I urge you to be patient, remain peaceful, accept the inevitable lows with the highs, equally embrace the successes with the failures, and learn from all your experiences that contentment, above all else, may be your greatest state of Grace. And one more thing: *learn to love.*

Further Information

Here are some useful websites for training and information:

In the UK

www.snu.org.uk The Spiritualist National Union, 'the largest Spiritualist organization in the world'. An ideal starting point for those in the UK.

www.spiritualistassociation.org.uk The Spiritualist Association of Great Britain – the other major source of information and routes for training in the UK.

www.arthurfindlaycollege.org The college offers courses to further mediumship skills.

www.nfsh.org.uk The National Federation of Spiritual Healers, UK – an excellent site with links, information and contacts for both UK and worldwide training in spiritual healing.

www.psychicnewsbookshop.co.uk The website of
Psychic News, the foremost British newspaper on psychic,
mediumistic and Spiritualist matters.

In the US and Canada

www.nsac.org The US National Spiritualist Association
of Churches – their website contains links, information
and news.

www.isa4usa.org The Independent Spiritualist
Association, USA – their site has listings of affiliated
churches in the US.

www.spiritualistchurchofcanada.com Gives links to
affiliated churches in Canada.

Worldwide

www.vsu.org.au/index.html The Victorian Spiritualists'
Union, Australia. The site gives a wide range of advice and
listings of centres all over Australia.

www.spiritualists.org.nz The Spiritualist Church of New
Zealand.

www.snui.org The new international branch of the UK's Spiritualist National Union, whose website is continually updated.

www.theisf.com/index.htm The International Spiritualist Federation – with a focus on research into spirit, they also give useful contacts.

www.spiritualist.tv Gives addresses and contact details for churches worldwide, as well as advice and information.

Also available by Gordon Smith

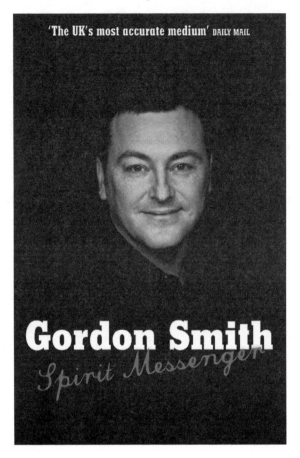

'The UK's most accurate medium' DAILY MAIL

Gordon Smith
Spirit Messenger

Read Gordon's first book, *Spirit Messenger*, and find out how he became a medium, what has influenced his spiritual development over the years and what it has been like to work with the scientific world. Full of numerous stories told in Gordon's down-to-earth style, *Spirit Messenger* is the beginning of the journey.

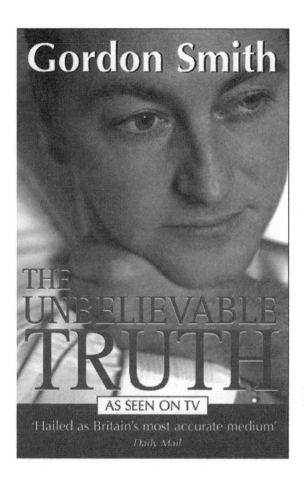

Gordon Smith

THE UNBELIEVABLE TRUTH

AS SEEN ON TV

'Hailed as Britain's most accurate medium'
Daily Mail

In this, Gordon's second book, he answers the questions he is most often asked by the people he meets. Gordon explains how the world of spirit works and how spirit communicates; he covers ghosts, hauntings, out-of-body experiences and much more. *The Unbelievable Truth* is ideal for anyone searching for more information on this huge subject area and is a perfect accompaniment to *Through My Eyes* and *Spirit Messenger*.

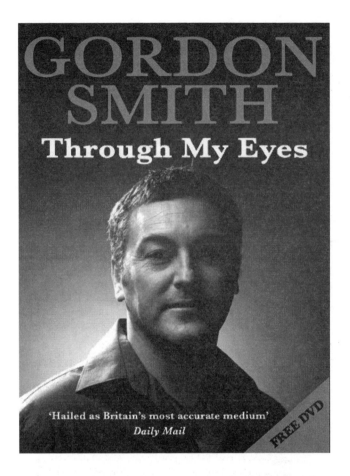

GORDON SMITH

Through My Eyes

'Hailed as Britain's most accurate medium'
Daily Mail

FREE DVD

Thousands of people have come to see Gordon seeking healing. From them he has gained a profound insight into the true nature of grief and our relationship with the spirit world. In his third book, join Gordon as he describes the true nature of grief, and how it affects us and our loved ones who have crossed over. An uplifting and insightful book guaranteed to bring peace of mind to anyone who has been touched by loss.

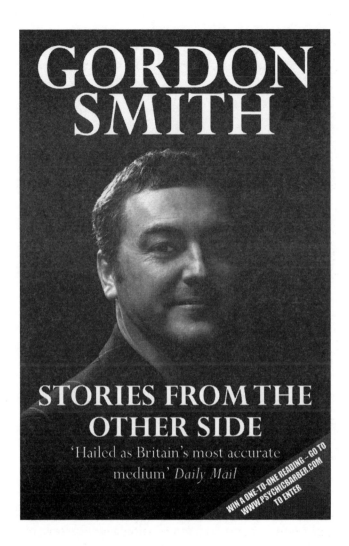

GORDON SMITH

STORIES FROM THE OTHER SIDE

'Hailed as Britain's most accurate medium' *Daily Mail*

This is Gordon's most personal and intimate book to date; in it he shares his experiences of growing up in Glasgow, his development as a medium and his extraordinary life working as a messenger for the spirit world.

GORDON SMITH

'Hailed as the UK's most accurate medium'
DAILY MAIL

Life
Changing
Messages

Remarkable stories from the other side

Join Gordon as he inspires and moves you once again.
In *Life-Changing Messages* Gordon allows people to
describe their experiences of his messages in their own
words and talks about how he brings these messages to
people, how they impact him and what he understands
about the nature of the other side.

GORDON SMITH

'Hailed as Britain's most accurate medium...'
The Daily Mail

THE AMAZING POWER OF ANIMALS

There have been many times when Gordon is giving a reading to a person about the loss of someone very close to them and the person cannot 'hear' the message – the pain has closed them down. But when an animal that they know turns up, the barriers just dissolve and they can accept the truth of the message that Gordon has given them about their loved ones. This book is full of astounding stories that are a great testimony to the power of animals and their unconditional love for us.

Gordon and his close friend Tibetan Buddhist and artist
Dronma have combined their skills and insights to create an
oracle that they hope will help people to live happier lives.
This extraordinary deck of oracle cards fuses ancient Tibetan
wisdom with contemporary Western psychological insight to
give you the keys to achieving a happier and more balanced
life. Using the five Tibetan elements of Earth, Water,
Fire, Air and Space, this deck will help you understand
the elemental forces, of which you and the world around
you are composed. Use these 34 cards for daily guidance,
individual spreads or meditation. Also included is a
mandala image for guidance in laying out spreads.

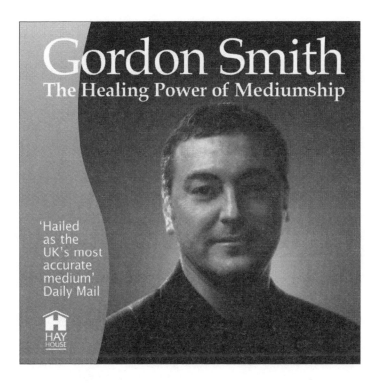

Gordon Smith
The Healing Power of Mediumship

'Hailed
as the
UK's most
accurate
medium'
Daily Mail

HAY
HOUSE

In this fascinating two-CD set, Gordon explains the role
of the medium in healing people's grief. The second CD
includes meditations to increase your ability to tune in
to the spirit world and send absent healing to anyone
who is in need.

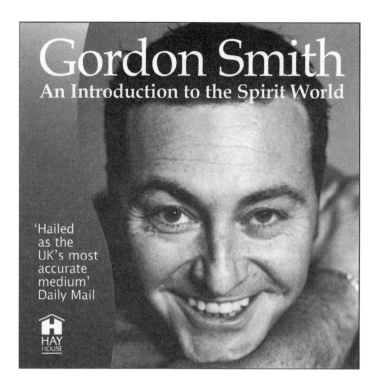

Gordon Smith
An Introduction to the Spirit World

'Hailed as the UK's most accurate medium'
Daily Mail

HAY HOUSE

On CD1 you can hear a live workshop in which Gordon describes his experiences of the spirit world and his development as a medium. He outlines the ways that the spirit world make their presence known to their loved ones and explains ways of feeling closer to spirit. In his down-to-earth and humorous style, Gordon explains some of the mechanics of mediumship and describes how psychics differ from mediums. Listening to this inspirational CD will enable you to gain a closer understanding of the work of a medium and help you to open up a deeper connection to the spirit world. CD2 contains three guided meditations:

1. Listening to your inner voice and higher self
2. Connecting to your spirit guides
3. Sending compassion and healing to others.

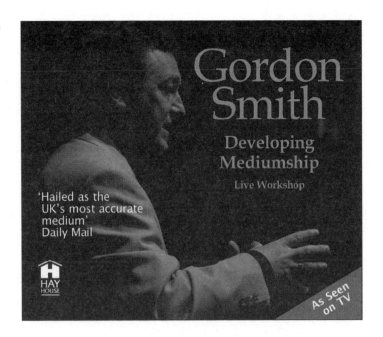

Let Gordon teach you how to begin to develop your connection with the spirit world and start to form a closer relationship with the spirits that are stepping forward to communicate with you.

Gordon will take you through meditations and exercises that will enable you to experience the difference between psychic ability and mediumship. In his warm and accessible style of teaching, Gordon will encourage you to take the first steps in increasing your spiritual awareness and to begin to trust the truth of your own experiences.

Don't forget you can find out more about Gordon Smith, his life, his work and his upcoming personal appearances by visiting his official website: www.psychicbarber.com

All of the above products are available from all good bookshops or by calling Hay House Publishers on 020 8962 1230

NOTES

NOTES

NOTES

NOTES

NOTES

Hay House Titles of Related Interest

ANGEL THERAPY
by Doreen Virtue

ASK YOUR GUIDES
by Sonia Choquette

*DAVID WELLS' COMPLETE GUIDE TO
DEVELOPING YOUR PSYCHIC SKILLS*
by David Wells

IT'S THE THOUGHT THAT COUNTS
by Dr David Hamilton

WHY MY MOTHER DIDN'T WANT ME TO BE PSYCHIC
by Heidi Sawyer

YOU CAN HEAL YOUR LIFE
by Louise L. Hay